3.29.94

Lech Wałęsa

Lech Wałęsa

Democrat or Dictator?

Jarosław Kurski

TRANSLATED BY

Peter Obst

Westview Press

BOULDER • SAN FRANCISCO • OXFORD

English edition copyright © 1993 by Westview Press, Inc. This translation has been revised and updated from the Polish original.

English edition published in 1993 in the United States of America by Westview Press, Inc., 5500 Central Avenue, Boulder, Colorado 80301-2877, and in the United Kingdom by Westview Press, 36 Lonsdale Road, Summertown, Oxford OX2 7EW

First published in Polish in 1991 by Wydawnictwo PoMOST as *Wódz* by Jarosław Kurski

Library of Congress Cataloging-in-Publication Data
Kurski, Jarosław, 1963–
   [Wódz. English]
   Lech Wałęsa: democrat or dictator? / Jarosław Kurski ; translated by Peter Obst.
      p.   cm.
   Includes bibliographical references and index.
   ISBN 0-8133-1788-6 — ISBN 0-8133-1789-4 (pbk.)
   1. Wałęsa, Lech. 1943–   . 2. Presidents—Poland—Biography.
3. Poland—Politics and government—1989–   . I. Title.
DK4452.W34K8713   1993
943.8—dc20   93-9886
                                                                                        CIP
                                                                                        AC

Printed and bound in the United States of America

The paper used in this publication meets the requirements
of the American National Standard for Permanence of Paper
for Printed Library Materials Z39.48-1984.

10   9   8   7   6   5   4   3   2   1

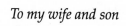

To my wife and son

*I will build democracy—democratically,
semidemocratically, and even undemocratically.*
                                    —Lech Wałęsa

Contents

Photographs

Translator's Note

When I first saw an excerpt from Jarosław Kurski's book in the Polish-language press in the United States, it did not occur to me that I would be the one to translate it into English. But it did make me take notice. For the first time someone was writing at length about the unknown side of Lech Wałęsa and presenting a most authoritative and fascinating picture. There was a certain irony in that it was the victory of Solidarity that had allowed uncensored press coverage in Poland, doing away with media that were very much a tool of the regime, often used to bolster the reputations of government officials. And yet between the time the media were given their freedom and the publication of the first criticism of Wałęsa, the press portrayed him in majestic, untouchable proportions, more like a plaster saint than a real human being. The ardor with which some journalists viewed Wałęsa was best demonstrated in an article written by a Polish reporter who interned at a U.S. newspaper. Deciding that the welcome given to Wałęsa by the local Polish-American community was not sufficiently rousing, the journalist wrote, "The city's Polish-Americans are proud of Lech Wałęsa and Solidarity. But not quite proud enough."[1] He then followed up with a list of other perceived shortcomings of the Poles living in the United States.

I made a mental note to acquire a copy of Kurski's book during a summer trip to Poland that I had already been planning. On my arrival in Warsaw, I found that my hosts—without knowing about my interest—had left a copy of the book in the room where I was to spend the night. Jet-lagged and not sleepy, I read most of it by the time the first rays of dawn lit up the city. Later, while in Kraków, I purchased my own copy at a bookstore I had long ago frequented while spending a summer at the Jagiellonian University. It was a much-changed place, a well-stocked, self-service store having replaced the one where surly clerks sold from a rather limited selection.

During a visit with relatives in Poznań, I mentioned the book to my cousin Radek Paciorek and commented that someone should translate it into English. In reply he asked if I would like to speak with Jarosław Kurski, the author. It turned out that he had met Kurski's brother Jacek

Wałęsa signing copies of *Wódz* at the Solidarity congress (photograph by Krzysztof Miller, *Gazeta Wyborcza*).

while working in the Solidarity underground press during the 1980s. (Radek had had many interesting experiences during those times, including being detained by the Communist militia for the possession of an unregistered typewriter.) I thought about this proposal; after all, cumulatively the articles I had translated during my freelance translating days easily exceed the length of two novels. I answered that I would at least like to talk with the author.

After many tries on Poland's highly challenging telephone network, I finally reached Jarosław Kurski in Gdańsk. Then on the last day of my trip, I met with his representative at an upscale Warsaw restaurant, and we reached an agreement. At that time I learned how controversial this book had been—and how popular, selling nearly 300,000 copies, of which 70,000 had been of a pirated edition. Outside of Poland it had been reviewed in the international editions of *Time* and *Newsweek*,[2] and rumor had it that the U.S. embassy had commissioned the translation of selected parts.

Later I learned that Wałęsa had read it—and obviously had not enjoyed it—during an airplane trip from Warsaw to Gdańsk. But with a smile on his face, he did autograph copies for attendees of the Solidarity congress in 1991.

I thus embarked on a project that proved both challenging and satisfying. Kurski's book was written in a lively style, a great improvement over the stilted newspaper prose of the articles I had translated before democracy arrived in Poland. But it did contain some colloquial expressions I was not familiar with. Fortunately, I was able to call on Alexandra and Stephen Medvec for assistance. I was further aided by Elżbieta Kulon, who verified the translation, while my sister, Ursula Obst, a professional editor and writer, used her sharp pencil on the English-language manuscript. My parents Bonifacy and Melania Obst gave their moral support to this enterprise, and my coworkers never ceased asking, "When will it ever be done?" I thank all of them.

Peter Obst

Lech Wałęsa (photograph by Anna Bohdziewicz, *Gazeta Wyborcza*).

Translator's Introduction

Be not afraid of greatness. Some are born great, some achieve greatness, and some have greatness thrust upon 'em.
—William Shakespeare, *Twelfth Night*, act 2, scene 5

Human lives are made up of turning points. For Wałęsa, like many a peasant's son, one such turning point came when he decided to leave the countryside and seek a better position in the city. He was well prepared. He had been much sought after as a farm-machinery mechanic; because of a shortage of spare parts, he had plenty of opportunities to develop his ability to improvise. In Gdańsk he found employment at the shipyard.

The Gdańsk shipyard, like the steel mills and coal mines, was one of the large industrial complexes on which socialistic Poland had staked its future. But it was different in several important aspects. Shipbuilding requires a high degree of skill, and the work, unlike that in the steel mills and coal mines, is nonrepetitive, as no two ships are ever identical in all details. It also takes a high level of organization to conduct and coordinate the complex activities that go into building a massive vessel that consists not just of a steel hull but the many mechanical systems that function within it.

In addition, the task of building ships demands not only craftsmanship but also a certain kind of self-sufficiency from each worker. Each may be required to function efficiently and in concert with others to complete every intricate task, sometimes under difficult circumstances. These conditions select for skilled and intelligent workers, but along with the skill and intelligence come increased expectations and a certain amount of intractability.

Wałęsa quickly adapted to the work environment and became popular with his coworkers. His ability to speak plainly and to the point, his resourcefulness, and his sincere religious convictions won the admiration of many in his work crew.

In 1970 protests broke out in Gdańsk as the government introduced across-the-board price increases. The militia was brought in, and many workers were killed by indiscriminate gunfire. This precipitated the fall of Władysław Gomułka's government and ushered in the one headed by

Edward Gierek. The new authorities moved to calm the situation. Gierek, the new Communist party secretary, capitalized on his blue-collar background (he had been a coal miner in Belgium and Poland) by coming to the shipyard to speak directly with the workers. Later, a meeting was organized in Warsaw with worker's delegates. Wałęsa, already involved in presenting the grievances of the strikers, was among those chosen to represent his fellow workers.

Gierek's administration rescinded the price increases but brushed aside many of the demands the workers made. The government embarked on a program that would use foreign loans to finance the rebuilding and modernization of Polish industry. The program was badly administered and eventually saddled the country with a multibillion-dollar foreign debt.

In 1976 further price hikes touched off another series of strikes. This time the workers in the cities of Radom and Ursus were at the core of the protest, with smaller strikes breaking out in other cities. A number of strikers were arrested and brutally treated by the militia. This gave rise to the formation of the Workers' Defense Committee (KOR), an organization whose purpose was to make the Polish authorities live up to the Helsinki agreement they had signed. In the same time period, legislative tinkering with the Polish constitution aimed at constraining citizens' rights and tightening the alliance with the Soviet Union drew protests from the intelligentsia and spawned a number of movements, including the "Flying University," a free, uncensored lecture circuit, and the Young Poland movement, which attracted many students. Among the workers, the Free Trade Union movement was born. Wałęsa was immediately drawn to it, because the Polish constitution gave workers the right to organize themselves into unions. By this time Wałęsa already had a reputation among his fellow workers as someone who had the common interest at heart and had proved himself worthy of their trust. Meanwhile, the official establishment had labeled him as a troublemaker.

The late 1970s brought a false feeling of prosperity to Poland. Outwardly it appeared that things were going well: Polish industry was being built up, and the amount of consumer goods on the market increased. But all this was a façade, as the export income to pay off the foreign loans was not materializing, and a financial crisis was in the making.

As the economic situation deteriorated in Poland during 1979, a popular and somewhat sensational book achieved best-seller status in the West. *The Third World War: August 1985*,[1] written by several ex-NATO functionaries, described a Soviet invasion of Europe that was triggered by strikes and civil unrest in Poland.

In August 1980, as the economic situation grew worse, workers on Poland's Baltic coast struck again, demanding not only higher wages to keep up with price increases but also changes in the relationship between the workers and the government, which controlled the huge industrial enterprises.

At the Gdańsk shipyards the strike was provoked by the firing of Anna Walentynowicz, a crane operator. The workers staged an in-place strike and occupied the facility, taking control of the gates. Wałęsa, who had been dismissed earlier, scrambled over a wall to join in the strike. He was elected to head the Interenterprise Strike Committee, which united the strike committees of several large government-run enterprises, and a list of demands was negotiated.

The list, which came to be known as the Twenty-one Demands, not only contained items relating to wages and working conditions but also called for access to information and the media, an end to the persecution of dissidents, the freeing of political prisoners, and the abolishment of privileges exercised by members of the Communist party and the security services.

The strike gained momentum. It became a united effort by workers who had the support of the intellectual community, the church, and Polish society at large. More than just a labor union, Solidarity had become a social movement. Many of Wałęsa's key advisors had been activists on behalf of democratic causes and brought their experience to the negotiations. As the strike talks continued, more and more members were signing on—many giving up their Communist party cards forever. Finally, the government gave in, and Solidarity became the first independent trade union in the Eastern bloc.

In some ways the strike was helped by the presence of the Western media, which to some extent prevented the Polish government from resorting to force and compelled it to negotiate in good faith. Almost overnight the press made Wałęsa a well-known figure around the world—and a national hero in Poland.

Plans were drawn to organize the various Solidarity groups across Poland, and for the formation of Rural Solidarity, a new organization for farmers. Wałęsa was elected as the first president of the labor union at the First National Solidarity Congress.

But the success of Solidarity lasted only 500 days. On December 13, 1981, General Wojciech Jaruzelski,[2] the first secretary of the Communist party and now head of the Polish government, imposed martial law and dissolved the Solidarity organization, substituting an officially sanctioned union as the only legitimate workers' organization. The army took command of the large population centers, patrolling the streets in armored cars. A curfew was established; transport and communications, both internal and external, were disrupted, causing severe shortages of food, fuel, and other daily necessities. Protests and strikes were crushed by the riot police. One particularly bloody action took place at the Wujek coal mine in Silesia, where tanks were brought in to dislodge protesters who had barricaded themselves on mine property.[3]

A wholesale arrest of Solidarity activists started. Interned in a country house in Arłamow, Wałęsa was kept isolated until November 1982. He was maintained in relative comfort and security, as the authorities were fearful of having any harm come to him. As Andrzej Gwiazda, an activist also imprisoned during this time, remarked, "I feel sorry for him because he is alone, but I do envy his conditions."[4]

Meanwhile, an underground Solidarity movement began to grow, keeping the resistance alive through underground newsletters and newspapers. Printed by volunteers who risked harsh prison sentences, these publications demonstrated to society at large that, in spite of the repression, the idea of independent trade unions and, ultimately, self-determination for the Polish people was far from crushed.

Although martial law was lifted in July 1983, many of its restrictive measures were incorporated into the civil code. Later that same year, Lech Wałęsa received the Nobel Peace Prize, which solidified his reputation at home and abroad and gave a much needed boost to the morale of the underground organization.

In October 1984 all of Poland was shocked by the news that a pro-Solidarity priest, Jerzy Popieluszko, had been murdered by the secret police, members of the department whose sole function was to monitor the movements of the clergy. For some time the government had been irritated by Popieluszko, whose sermons on human dignity and individual courage in the face of adversity were reaching an ever-growing audience. His murder was a sober reminder of the true nature of the ruling regime.

In 1986 the government declared a general amnesty for those who had been arrested, and it released 20,000 detainees, including many of the top Solidarity activists. But by this time Polish society was worn down, dispirited, and uncertain. Few believed that Wałęsa, or anyone else, could do anything to change the situation. In a remarkably perceptive article written in 1986, U.S. journalist P. J. O'Rourke captured the prevailing climate in Poland. He quoted a Polish music critic—a man close to his country's moods—who said, after someone mentioned Wałęsa, "No one cares about that any more. It's old history. Only people from the West think it means anything any more."[5]

In early 1987 the United States rescinded the last of the trade sanctions it had imposed on Poland at the onset of martial law. The year also brought a third papal visit, and spirits of the Polish people started to rise.

Later, Vice-President George Bush visited Poland and by seeking out Wałęsa further reinforced the belief that there was concern abroad for the Polish situation.

Desperate for public support, the Polish government held a referendum hoping to win popular approval for a new, stern economic program. Solidarity, trying to establish itself as a viable power center, called for a boycott of the referendum and was successful.

With the economy of Poland in shambles and strikes breaking out around the country, the Jaruzelski government reached an impasse. At the same time Solidarity leaders were calling for negotiations in a round-table format and the relegalization of their union.

In November 1988 a debate was held on Polish television featuring Alfred Miodowicz, the head of the "official" labor union, and Lech Wałęsa, the onetime head of the still officially disbanded, though in reality very much alive, Solidarity. Wałęsa had put enormous effort into preparations for his appearance. His advisors supplied him with all the information that he might need, including tips on how to handle the hot television lights. After seven years in obscurity, Wałęsa came in front of the Polish public and presented a clear case for change in Poland. Soon after, the government started taking a serious approach to the idea of the Round Table negotiations.

Members of the Communist government on one side and Lech Wałęsa and the Solidarity leadership on the other hammered out an agreement to share power in parliament. Elections were to be held. Up for grabs were 100 seats in the newly created upper house, the senate (or Senat), and 35 percent of the seats in the Sejm, the lower house (the remainder were to be reserved for the incumbent regime).

Solidarity mobilized all its resources for the coming elections. Under the new relaxed regulations, Adam Michnik and other Solidarity underground journalists organized a newspaper, the *Gazeta Wyborcza* (Election gazette). All of Polish society was involved in the campaign. Walls were covered with posters (a common medium of communication that the Poles have made into an art form) announcing various candidates. One popular Solidarity poster featured a black-and-white still photo of Gary Cooper from *High Noon*, his sheriff's badge replaced by the red-and-white Solidarity logo.

Solidarity and allied candidates claimed all the seats except for one in the senate, which went to an independent candidate. One Polish citizen commented on the process, "Before we were made to vote [in single-slate elections]; now we can actually elect someone."

Tadeusz Mazowiecki, a veteran politician from the Catholic opposition group Znak (Sign), was appointed as prime minister. The newly created post of president was given to Jaruzelski. Wałęsa resumed his position as the head of a reborn Solidarity labor union. In November 1989 he traveled to Canada, Venezuela, and the United States, where he addressed a joint session of Congress. The first words of his speech, "We the people," brought forth a flood of applause.

In January 1990 the Polish United Workers' party was dissolved. In October Jaruzelski stepped down from the presidency and into retirement. In the subsequent presidential elections there were three dominant candidates: Wałęsa, Mazowiecki, and Stanisław Tymiński, a Polish emigré businessman. No candidate achieved majority in the first vote; after a runoff election against Tymiński, Wałęsa become Poland's president.

This book covers events that took place from July 1989 through March 1992. It presents a close-up portrait of Wałęsa using the words of those who worked closely with him.

P. O.

Introduction

In the "year of Mazowiecki,"[1] Lech Wałęsa was like a fish washed up on the sand. To survive politically he had to change into a scorpion.

October and November 1989 marked the height of Wałęsa's popularity in Poland and around the world. In international circles he was still regarded as Poland's foremost citizen and a great symbol of the struggle against totalitarianism. But in the months that followed, Wałęsa's popularity at home started to slip as his myth was placed under close scrutiny. Suddenly he was no longer a political arbitrator but the fomenter of conflict. In the minds of many he was no longer the architect of a new democratic order but its devastator.

In the new circumstances his personal characteristics, once secondary, became annoying. At one time everyone turned a blind eye toward them. After all, what were the few bad habits and weaknesses of one man against the challenge of defeating Communist totalitarianism? The personal desires and ambitions of the Solidarity leader had almost always run counter to the desires and aspirations of Polish society. From the moment that the non-Communist government was formed, the interests of Lech Wałęsa were no longer one with those of Poland. When the natural enemy of Solidarity, the PZPR (Polish United Workers' party—the Communist party), dissolved, Wałęsa's new number-one opponent became Prime Minister Tadeusz Mazowiecki, who received his appointment on August 24, 1989. To exist and to justify his intense activity, Wałęsa decided to use the rhetoric of fear, uncertainty, and danger. First he started to talk about the smell of gunpowder in the street, then he started his "war at the top," lashing out at high-ranking officials he had previously treated with special care. In particular, he ended his cautious approach in dealing with General Wojciech Jaruzelski—then Poland's president—and abandoned his circumspect treatment of matters relating to the USSR. He no longer picked his words carefully but opened up full blast. He managed to alienate most of his old advisors. In a few months he created an army of opponents, thus assuring himself of work for years to come. How many battles, how many wars and campaigns would have to be fought to defeat them all? Now he had a goal and sense of purpose.

The new slogan that Lech put on the banners (and that was the required ideology for all his supporters) addressed the struggle with the monopoly of Solidarity.[2]

The span of time during which I worked for Lech as a press spokesman (October 20, 1989–July 9, 1990) encompassed both his crisis and his triumph. But by becoming a press spokesman I did not cease to be a journalist. Providence gave me the opportunity to take a close look at a man who in the next several years will exert an enormous influence on Polish society. A journalist cannot waste a chance like this. Poles should be able to view a multifaceted portrait of their president, one without blank spaces or touch-ups. This is why this book was born. I kept notes as events took place; I trust, therefore, that my writing serves as an authentic record.

In Wałęsa's presence I was never able to find the humility to disregard my own convictions. But cooperation with Lech requires complete faith in the greatness and wisdom of the chief—or the ability, like that of a full-blooded politician, to adjust to any set of circumstances. But if one stays faithful to one's own convictions and sense of decorum, unexpected things can happen. First there is a period of severe turbulence—then good-byes are exchanged. That is, of course, if one hands in the resignation in time. Otherwise one is bounced upstairs or sideways.

In order not to be accused of being faithless and lacking in respect and called worse (try: traitor, turncoat, mean-spirited, mischief-maker, frustrated liar, and God knows what else) by the most ardent among Wałęsa's followers, I should have published this book fifty years after my own death. I would probably have done that very thing had I felt the book would in any way interfere with the rules of fair play. The passions generated during the presidential election campaign of 1990 were not favorable to early publication. I did not wish to become embroiled in the political struggle around the persona of the future president. If the book were published before the election it would no doubt be a hot item, but this would degrade it to a mere propaganda piece.

Wałęsa is the subject of many books. But most of them were written by those who approached the subject on their knees and who had been appointed to carry out such a project. These books range from high-sung praises of the chief's genius to works that resemble an account of the life of a saint. Until this day the most accurate portrait of Wałęsa is contained in the 1981 essay "A Man of What Substance?" by Lech Bądkowski (which appears at the end of this book).

I attribute Wałęsa's favorable treatment by the press (except the lies and propaganda spread by the Communists) to the social syndrome of what Bądkowski called the "hunger for moral leadership." As Bądkowski wrote, "this hunger ... caused Wałęsa to be elevated to incredible heights,

Wałęsa can be a most dynamic individual, literally and figuratively (photographs by Anna Bohdziewicz, *Gazeta Wyborcza*).

4

One moment he is one person, the next another (photographs by Anna Bohdziewicz, *Gazeta Wyborcza*).

and in this case we cannot try to sober up the populace, because we would be depriving them of the very thing for which they fought so hard, and received with such joy." During the years of martial law (1981–1983) Wałęsa became a national legend. He was the subject of attack by a rabid Communist propaganda machine. At that time no one (besides a few anarchistic youth groups) would help the Communists by attempting to criticize Wałęsa. But at that time his behavior did not warrant critique.

Criticism first appeared only in 1990, about three months after his triumphal visit to the United States. With the Communist threat gone for good—defeated by Lech himself—the silence about Lech's negative characteristics was broken. The journalists, tired of his behavior, began to expose the man who was, until then, an unassailable national icon. Newspaper articles about Walesa became more interesting, and more skeptical.

My job as a press spokesman[3] was to preserve a positive image of the chief in the media and in the social consciousness. It was about as easy and enjoyable as riding a bicycle on a high wire without a safety net—while playing the violin.

This book is an attempt to portray Lech in motion. He is a most dynamic individual, literally and figuratively. One moment he is one person, the next another. He can be placed in front of a camera and a snapshot made. But such a portrait always only shows a part of the truth. And rather than trying to "assemble" him from a series of such photographs it would be better to film him in action—from the top, sides, bottom, front, and back—and then simply show the film.

Well, let's get started. Lights … !

If my countrymen place me upon this pedestal then I will ask all my colleagues from the KK [Solidarity National Commission] to Belweder Palace and say that it was a wave of solidarity that brought me there. Then, at a common table, we will quickly choose a new leader for the labor union.

> —Lech Wałęsa, at the Second National Solidarity Congress, immediately after his election as chairman, April 1990

December 22, 1990: A column of automobiles pulls up in front of Belweder Palace,[1] the location of the president's office. The first one disgorges Lech Wałęsa and his spouse. He is greeted in the traditional Polish manner, with bread and salt. He ascends the steps. Strobes flash; the guards salute. He crosses the shining marble floor. The double doors of the presidential suite swing open as he approaches. The president enters. The "court" trailing behind him halts at the door. All have worked long and hard to be there. A sea of faces mirrors the satisfaction of the moment during which Lech takes his seat behind the executive desk. He leans on his outstretched arms. He takes a look at his surroundings. On this day his term of office begins ...

Eight months earlier—April 10—was judgment day. The world press had prematurely reported that Wałęsa intended to seek the presidential office. This "Black Tuesday" will probably remain the most instructive day of my journalistic career.

The announcement came about from the intense desire, on the part of both society and the media, for this very story. The news-hungry press gave weight to Lech's frequent but unclear pronouncements that he did not wish to be president, but ... if the situation forced him and society asked him to, then he would consent—though in truth he did not want to do it. The media's appetite increased when Jarosław Kaczyński, a political advisor to Wałęsa, gave an interview that appeared in the previous Saturday's *Życie Warszawy* (Warsaw life), a popular Warsaw daily newspaper.

According to Kaczyński, "Wałęsa's presidency is not an end in itself. It is the effect resulting from the exhaustion of the present political alignment. In my opinion under the current government we cannot move forward, and we certainly cannot make sufficient headway; that is why I think that Wałęsa could become president even without the planned elections."

A similar interview appeared in the Monday (April 9) edition of *Gazeta Gdańska* (Gdańsk gazette). The subject of the interview, in this case, was the twin brother of Jarosław, Leszek Kaczyński, vice-chairman of Solidarity. These two interviews by representatives of the same political camp, published at nearly the same time, could be interpreted only in one way: as the start of a political offensive launched by Lech's advisors with his unspoken consent.

Two days later, while the entire world was commenting on the subject of presidential candidate Wałęsa, Leszek Kaczyński, shaking his head with disbelief at the enormity of the forces he had unleashed, declared that he had not coordinated anything with his brother, that he only read his brother's interview after giving his own, and that there was no likelihood of beginning a presidential campaign. He was also aware that any premature revelations about a presidential campaign would have an unfavorable effect on Wałęsa's popularity and on the undertaking as a whole.

The following week the balloon was stretched to its limits. On Tuesday it ruptured in two places.

The First Rupture

Jagienka Wilczak, a reporter for the weekly journal *Polityka* (Politics)[2] came to the Akwen, the building where Solidarity offices were located, to gather material for an article about the coming Solidarity congress. She conducted several interviews with important officials of the union. She also found her way to Krzysztof Pusz, Wałęsa's personal secretary.

Pusz is crude, kindhearted, and understanding. He made his money on tie-dyed jeans. During martial law the Communists took his store. But he continued to be active in the underground union movement. He is generous and free with money. He loves pig's feet and cognac. He dresses flamboyantly, like a gypsy king. He answers most questions with a single sentence. He plays close to his vest and does not go looking for awards.

Word by word Wilczak worked her way to questions about the presidency. This was a topic widely discussed in Lech's presence, and Pusz, forgetting himself, treated the reporter to several spicy details. It so happened that the ever-present Ryszard Wesołowski, a stringer for Reuters (who carefully divides his loyalty between his friends and his profession), was hanging around the office, as he usually did, for days at a time. Hearing this he burst into the office like a bat out of hell, screaming, "What! You give information to [the formerly Communist] *Polityka* but not to Reuters?!"

Pusz, the very personification of goodness and trust, decided to share a few of his own opinions. The Reuters Warsaw correspondent, Michał Broniatowski, immediately called for a statement. Pusz blazed away without in the least considering that his words would later become the material for a hot Reuters story: "At the Solidarity Congress Wałęsa should again be chosen as chairman of the organization. Two or three weeks later he should resign and name his successor. Then with the affirmed mandate and support from society at large he should declare his readiness to run for the presidency. Jaruzelski should then resign, and if he would not then he should be forced out."

At 3 p.m. I received a call from a journalist who asked for a comment on Pusz's statement. I asked him to read it to me, explaining that our office was not hooked up to the Reuters news service. When I heard the statement, beads of perspiration burst out on my forehead. I managed to avoid making any further comments by stating that I was Wałęsa's press spokesman, not his secretary.

The Second Rupture

During the hectic investigation into what actually happened, I received a call from Staszek Turnau, a former colleague now employed at Poland's national daily newspaper, the *Gazeta Wyborcza* (Election gazette), who told me of a remark Lech supposedly made to the Polish Press Agency (PAP). The PAP correspondent had asked Wałęsa to confirm the statement that Jarosław Kaczyński had given earlier to *Życie Warszawy*, that Wałęsa was going to seek the presidency. Wałęsa answered: "We must speed up the tempo of reform, change the old alignments. The Kaczyński brothers have done me a disservice. They spoke too soon; it could cost me the election, but that is freedom of the press. Yes, I confirm the statement."

The telephones continued to ring. The first calls came from accredited foreign correspondents in Poland, later calls from the world at large. I could not believe what was happening. It was impossible to make a comment. The entire situation was absurd. It reduced a serious political concept to the level of a momentary media sensation. I decided to call Wałęsa immediately to tell him what was happening. Wałęsa exploded. "I didn't confirm anything; it's a lie. You must issue a counterstatement. Someone is putting me on," he yelled into the receiver. "Some woman accosted me on the steps, then came to the conference. I answered her, but in a very noncommittal manner—she didn't even have a tape recorder. It wasn't an official statement."

I refused to issue a counterstatement because I felt that it just would not do the job. For one reason, I was sure that it would not be credible because I expected that Anna Stokrocka, the PAP editor, would have a recording of the conversation with Wałęsa. For another, no one would have believed such a counterstatement. And finally, such an action would have been a last resort that, in my opinion, was much overused by Lech.

The day this happened the meeting of the KKW (the Solidarity Executive Committee) presidium had been held in the large meeting room on the ground floor of the Akwen, and not (as usual) in the conference room near Lech's office. The chief had gone down. I was overwhelmed with work and had no intention of running from floor to floor. The damaging statement was given in the stairwell practically on the run. Lech, like Pusz in speaking with the Reuters correspondent, did not realize the harm his words would do.

If the KKW presidium had not had its meeting that day, then the PAP journalist would not have been there. If the meeting had taken place upstairs, rather than downstairs, then Wałęsa would not have made the unfortunate remark. If not for the journalist from *Polityka* and the omnipresent Reuters stringer, Pusz would not have made his comment. If, if …

Even though the pinprick had come at the end of a string of coincidences, the balloon would eventually have burst anyway. It was at the breaking point and had to give. It simply would have popped at a different place and a different time.

Loyalty Is Not Lech's Strong Suit

I don't know what shook Leszek Kaczyński more—the confirmation of Lech's desire to seek the presidency or the crack about his disserving. In a statement issued to PAP, I tried to smooth things over: "The question of the PAP journalist concerned the next presidential election whose timing and rules have not yet been settled. So far no steps have been taken except those allowed by the constitution. In this light we must view Lech Wałęsa's statements. The opinions of Leszek and Jarosław Kaczyński are not at odds with those of the Solidarity leader." At the request of Lech and Leszek, to erase any bad impressions, I added, "The brothers Kaczyński and Lech Wałęsa continue to work together."

Leszek Kaczyński is a man of incredible industriousness, knowledge and uncommon intelligence. He spends days in his office, chain smoking. When immersed in conversation he is so involved that he forgets about his cigarette until it burns down, singeing his fingers. In shaking off the ashes, he always misses the ashtray. Sitting at the edge of his chair, he slips into a near-crouching position while murmuring things that are both intelligent and interesting. He is not only the vice-chairman of the union but its finest brain. Politics is his element, as it is for his brother, Jarosław. A strike by the brothers would have left Solidarity floundering.

This day I realized that the symbiotic relationship between Lech and the Kaczyński brothers was founded not on mutual trust, respect, or loyalty but on shared interests and political pragmatism. Wałęsa was the motive power for the brothers, their engine and billboard. Meanwhile, the Kaczyńskis gave Wałęsa the necessary ideology to justify his actions and ambitions.

Wałęsa often consciously failed to inform the Kaczyńskis about his plans or even about things he already had done. Leszek learned about the dismissal of Henryk Wujec and Adam Michnik after the fact. It was the same with Wałęsa's July meeting with the prime minister and the settling of the Słupsk rail strike, about which Leszek heard on the radio. Wałęsa's statement supporting the election of a president by a popular vote over having him chosen by the parliament—which went counter to one of the points in the Center Alliance party platform—reached Leszek through the daily press. He called Wałęsa to complain. Wałęsa (I know from Pusz) gave him an earful back.

Politics is Lech's personal province. Whoever thinks that Lech is influenced by his advisors is wrong. Even when Wałęsa does exactly what his advisors want him to do, it does not mean that he does not know what he is doing. He has full control despite any appearance of dependence. He is not sentimental, does not become fond of anyone, but treats all the workers in his office pragmatically and dispassionately. Everyone is expendable; there are no alliances that cannot be broken. The advisors merely play the role of informers and living sources of knowledge.

Jacek Merkel, Wałęsa's close associate, thinks that Leszek Kaczyński believes in the fiction that Wałęsa can be surrounded by a group people (real authorities, not sycophants) who, working in conjunction, can force him to do certain things. Wałęsa will always break out of such an arrangement if he is convinced that it is too confining. One of Merkel's colleagues has said that the difference between Wałęsa and Marshal Józef Piłsudski, Poland's prewar leader, lies in that Piłsudski was always loyal to his lieutenants, never abandoned them. Piłsudski's people were one with the marshal. This is not Wałęsa's way.

Leszek Kaczyński should know this. He himself has stated, "I have no delusions about the fact that Lech will play me off against my brother. I know him. ... My friends and colleagues ask, 'Are you aware that Lech may dump you?' I am well aware of this. I like Lech in my own way but have no doubt that even if he likes me, he will not hold back from doing what he feels must be done."

On the day following "Black Tuesday," Jacek Moskwa, then assistant editor of *Rzeczpospolita* (Commonwealth), came to Gdańsk to interview

Wałęsa for his government daily. The interview appeared April 17, 1990, under the title "A Finger into the Fire" and was intended to calm the raging waters of public opinion. The article was done in two stages (Wałęsa gave Moskwa carte blanche): First Moskwa interviewed the chief in his office, then he interviewed Leszek Kaczyński.

Wałęsa was quoted as saying, "My statement was taken literally. I am happy to hear that there is a social need for such discussion. But it is not good that it is being used to drive a wedge between me and my friends. Among those I number Jarosław and Leszek Kaczyński. They suggested this matter. Very well then, may all of Poland have a discussion, with me as the subject."

It is worthwhile to quote a few typical reactions from the world press, which was unaware that the statement about Walesa's candidacy was essentially a false start. There was some interesting speculation on the timing and the reasons for the announcement.

On April 10, 1990, the *Washington Post* quoted Jarosław Kaczyński: "'Nobody is talking about a date for elections or about starting any procedures,' he [Kaczyński] said. 'He [Wałęsa] just states a certain fact' that he will run when Jaruzelski leaves office."

On April 11, the *San Francisco Chronicle* carried the following story:

> Solidarity leader Lech Wałęsa yesterday declared his intention to run for the presidency of Poland, the first step in an apparent campaign to force President Wojciech Jaruzelski from office. ...
>
> Jaruzelski did not respond to Wałęsa's move, and his reaction to it was not known. The revelation came on the eve of Jaruzelski's official visit to the Soviet Union. The four-day trip will be particularly significant because Moscow is expected to admit culpability for the murder of thousands of Polish officers in the Katyń Forest during World War II.

In the view of some observers the timing of his announcement was an attempt to take away some of the political impact which Jaruzelski could gain from the trip.

On the same day the *Los Angeles Times* wrote, "Pusz, chief of Wałęsa's secretariat, told reporters that Wałęsa should become president soon because Jaruzelski was doing nothing to speed up reforms at home or win help for Poland from abroad. 'Everything is going too slowly. We need someone with a whip,' he said."

Several commentators in the mass media questioned Wałęsa's ability to be president, stating that his open combative style would not suit him well as a head of state.

On April 12, the *New York Times* reported:

Mr. Wałęsa told reporters in Gdańsk, his hometown, that his remarks to several journalists about running for President had merely been "a metaphor" aimed at accelerating the pace of his country's political reforms.

"The slogan in which I say Lech Wałęsa is ready to run for President means that he wants to speed up reforms, so that the reforms are quicker and better, not that Lech Wałęsa wants to be President," said the Solidarity founder, who sometimes refers to himself in the third person.

Elsewhere Wałęsa was quoted saying that he "would not run away" if the citizens of Poland wished him to be president.

On April 12 at a meeting in Elbląg, he criticized Jaruzelski and separated himself from the "eggheads" who speak foreign languages.

Few Poles doubted that Wałęsa would indeed seek the presidency, as seemed confirmed in the opening minutes of the press conference. Wałęsa was there ten minutes before the announced starting time, sat at the podium, and invited members of the union to present copies of his book *A Way of Hope* for an autograph. "Please come up," he said, "I will not have time for this after I become president."

There is no doubt Wałęsa's presidential campaign began on April 10 and lasted almost eight months. In the first phase, before Wałęsa formally announced his candidacy, he went about explaining the Polish voters' immaturity within the democratic process as an institutionalized form. He liked to point out that when children in the United States pick a class president, there are always several willing contenders. In Poland, meanwhile, the class president is dragged out of the crowd by the ears. Wałęsa knew that he could not say, "I want to be president." He, too, wanted to be dragged into office by his ears, pushed by the masses, the working people from cities and villages. He spoke about another aspect of the presidency, playing up to the reporters a little. "Presidents Bush or Mitterrand, for example," he said, "are the least free persons on the face of the earth. When I worked at the shipyard I could drop my screwdriver and pliers at the end of the day and enjoy my freedom. A president can't even get a good night's sleep because he knows that his security force is checking if his snoring is regular. I don't want to be president; I want to be a free man the way I once was." Later the campaign took on the typical forms found in the democratic countries of the West. Yet Merkel, Wałęsa's campaign secretary, now thinks that in the beginning his chief did not want to bind the campaign within traditional limits.

Yet the first, quiet echoes about Wałęsa's candidacy appeared in the Western press even before Lech betrayed any intention to that effect. The harbinger was the Warsaw meeting that failed to happen, between Vaclav Havel and Wałęsa. The Czechoslovakian president arrived in Warsaw on

January 25, 1990, for one day only, with the intention of meeting just about everyone. Before his departure for Poland he supposedly mentioned his readiness to meet Wałęsa in Gdańsk. This idea, in view of the short duration of his visit, was unrealistic. The organizers, however, assured Havel that Wałęsa would come to Warsaw. This proved too much for Wałęsa. He was adamant. He said that he would never go.

The telephones rang off the hook. Mazowiecki called three times to beg him to come. Bronisław Geremek, a trusted advisor, called several times. Michnik, a longtime opposition activist and Solidarity supporter, now the editor of *Gazeta Wyborcza*, called as well. But it was to no avail. Wałęsa said that those in Warsaw were trying to manipulate him. He said that he had a rally at the shipyard and would not change his plans at the last minute. I explained to the press that the meeting would not take place because of a clash of schedules and technical difficulties. I told them that Wałęsa had great respect for Havel and that ambition or animosity did not enter the picture, as the press suggested. I also added that Wałęsa would very much like to meet with Havel, was convinced that sooner or later such a meeting would take place, and would prefer that it occur in Gdańsk, the birthplace of Solidarity.

I lied—of course I lied. Yes, there was a rally at the shipyard and some technical difficulties, but that was only a part of the truth. Wałęsa's frequent criticism of Havel led me to believe that at the core of it all lay envy and ambition caused by Wałęsa's desire for the victor's laurels—for being the first to break out of Moscow's grip. In addition Havel's schedule in Warsaw was packed, and Wałęsa would have been only one of many people meeting Havel on his run from the Council of Ministers to the Sejm,[3] and the Belweder Palace. Lech did not know Havel personally, but he did say that the same parliament that had once sent Havel to prison later unanimously chose him as president. He was galled by the fact that Havel was given the presidency after a few successful demonstrations, whereas he would now have to struggle and sweat to attain the same goal. Not without some reason did he say, "Now they are clapping for Havel, but soon he will get booed. Wait until our car [the economy] gets going. At this time it is stalled, but the Czechs are going in reverse."

Lech's sensitivity was not salved even by an article in *Le Monde* (February 23, 1990) describing Havel's visit to the United States.

> The enthusiasm during the reception given by both houses of Congress to greet Vaclav Havel was only vaguely reminiscent to that created by an earlier visitor—Lech Wałęsa, a common citizen. It was not like the excitement that Wałęsa unleashed, though it was more than the merely polite reaction of indifferent congressmen.

[Havel, unlike Wałęsa, did not ask for American money, but said that he desired a Europe without either Soviet or American troops.]

Many politicians in Washington, especially Vice-president Dan Quayle, who remained ice cold to Havel's words, did not share this viewpoint. Havel did manage to suppress the worst inferences of that statement by joking that it is not as if Vaclav Havel the writer would dissolve the Warsaw Pact on one day and NATO on the next. Some members of the American government did say as an aside that the Czechoslovak president gave them the impression of being a harmless dreamer, a romantic, and somewhat naïve, rather than a genuine head of government.

Later, when activists from the Polish-Czechoslovak Solidarity group arrived in Gdańsk with a proposal to set things right again, with a lot of attendant publicity, Lech agreed immediately.

Both Wałęsa and Havel took helicopters for the final leg of the trip to their meeting in the Karkonosze Mountains on the Polish-Czech border on March 17, 1990. Someone jokingly suggested that between them—the electrician Wałęsa and chemist Havel (by virtue of his university degree)—they had started the catalysis necessary to charge the batteries. For the core of Solidarity activists, Zbigniew Bujak, Władysław Frasyniuk, Bronisław Geremek, Zbigniew Janas, Adam Michnik, Jan Lityński, and Janusz Onyszkiewicz, this was the last meeting during which they sat on the same side of the table with Wałęsa.

The weather was gorgeous. The snow was melting in the springtime sun, while the place chosen for its remoteness and quiet became a mecca for hundreds of reporters and photojournalists. When Havel arrived he was surrounded by a sea of hysterical Czechs. Everyone and everything was stepped upon. Abandoned skis cracked underfoot; fashionable ski outfits were torn. The masters of the situation were those photographers who had two cameras—one for taking pictures and one for pounding the heads of rivals. The crowd around Wałęsa was just as thick. Each leader was surrounded by a disorderly mass of flesh. It took them a quarter of an hour to find each other. Wałęsa was injured by some sharp instrument. In the Spindlerova Bouda, a ski chalet on the Czech side of the border, Havel declared that this improvised struggle was proof of true, undeclared Polish-Czech friendship.

For his part, Wałęsa said, "I must apologize that we did not get to meet earlier in Warsaw. But I am a practical man and to the point. Because you met with my colleagues while on a one-day visit to Warsaw, I did not look at the circumstances, at the symbolic meanings. And this caused me some troubles. It was widely interpreted that it was due to ambition, that there was a misunderstanding—but there was nothing to it. That's the

Vaclav Havel and Lech Wałęsa posing for photographers (photograph by Krzysztof Miller, *Gazeta Wyborcza*).

work of the intellectuals. I am a worker; I am not able to think these things up. "

First they decided on the press release, and then they sat down to talk. The strange order of the two actions came out of a tradition dating back to 1978, when Havel, Jacek Kuroń (one of the founders of KOR, the Workers' Defense Committee), Michnik, and Lityński met for the first time without Wałęsa. Disbelieving their success at coming together and fearing the Communist security services would disrupt the meeting, they decided to establish proof of their accomplishment: They composed a press release and held the meeting afterward. The meeting in the Karkonosze Mountains gave Lech the opportunity to see that Havel was a modest man, more ethical than political, without active aspirations to become the first reformer of the Eastern bloc. Havel is a singular personality. I got the impression that during the first part of the discussion Wałęsa was sounding out his partner. When the trials were over and Wałęsa had a positive result, his doubts disappeared; he felt that he was the dominant figure. The discussion started making sense, and even though they were cast from different molds, the two men liked each other.

On the return trip Wałęsa admitted that Havel was a regular guy. Direct confirmation of this feeling was the way Wałęsa answered a question at the press conference held later. The reporter asked whether Poland or Czechoslovakia was further along in its reforms. Wałęsa dodged the issue: "The point of view depends on where you sit. There are some areas where Poland leads, but on the question of the presidency the Czechs are definitely ahead."

Up to that time such a provocative question would have elicited the standard answer: "Poland is first! All that has happened is because of us! I have heard it said that it took Poland ten years to win its freedom, that it took Hungary ten months, East Germany ten weeks, and Czechoslovakia ten days. But such statements are merely political posturing. The Czech revolution was possible only because of Poland." I am deeply convinced that if Havel had not had a positive effect on Wałęsa, nothing would have stopped him from using this answer (which, after all, does contain a great deal of truth). Geremek knew this, too. He had taken the trouble to travel to the Karkonosze Mountains through Gdańsk so as to have an opportunity to convince Wałęsa about Havel's good intentions. All who knew Lech went to the Spindlerova Bouda with some dread. During the trip to the meeting Wałęsa had given an interview to Gdańsk TV aboard the aircraft and had stated that there are many naïve people in Czechoslovakia who think that it takes just ten days to make a revolution.

A few days before the uproar about the presidency, during the weekend of April 7–8, a meeting took place at the Gdańsk residence of the influential Bishop Tadeusz Gocłowski, who had served as mediator in previous political disputes. The purpose of the meeting was to smooth out some of the conflicts growing within Solidarity and to persuade Lech not to pursue early elections for the presidency. Along with the host, the top politicians of Solidarity—Geremek, Aleksander Hall, Michnik, Piotr Nowina-Konopka, Jan Olszewski, Andrzej Stelmachowski, Mazowiecki, and of course Wałęsa—were gathered.

The meeting was shrouded in secrecy. Lech was not swayed on a single point. No one questioned Lech's candidacy. They talked only about the timing. "Lech, not now; wait till spring [1991]!" But Lech remained unconvinced—firing off replies like a machine gun. "Gentlemen," he said, "I will be president whether you wish it or not. It was even decided that professor Geremek should be vice-president even though there is no provision for such an office in the constitution. Meanwhile Tadeusz Mazowiecki will remain as prime minister."

Aleksander Hall: Wałęsa's presidency would have been the natural fulfillment of the democratic process in Poland and would have fallen into his lap of its own accord. That is why no one among the elite questioned it at first. No one said no. The fact that there were people who eventually did say no is closely linked to Lech's attitude during that whole year. The deciding factor was Lech's switch to promoting his own ambitions over the common good. I am certain that a Lech who calmly, majestically viewed the events around him would have arrived at the presidency without any internal discord. It was the way things had to go.

The Second National Solidarity Congress,[4] like the first, took place at the Oliwia sports arena in Gdańsk. Lech's comments about his bid for the presidency contributed much to setting the overall tone and dominated the news coming out of the congress. True, he never addressed this subject directly, but it was ever-present in his speeches.

For example, he would say:

> Many thought that the worker [as leader] was accidental. It was an accident that would not fit into the heads of the intellectuals. Today when I have put the presidency out as bait they are saying—just hear them—that I don't have the appearance for it. This means that if you are an intellectual you wear a tie, a bow tie, and formal clothes—but if you are a worker then you put on overalls. This is one comment. Another is that I should speak better, but most of all that I should read the things they write for me. But I have a third principle, gentlemen, and that is to get things done.

Lech, stressing that he would not speak French (the onetime language of diplomacy), fell into anti-intellectual rhetoric, inscribing forever the expression *egghead intellectuals* into his political vocabulary. And yet he answered one of the final questions at a later press conference with the following remark. "No one can catch up to Wałęsa. I am self-taught. At this moment I am a driver [leader of the labor union] but I have started to read out loud at home and later will speak correctly and with good diction."

His consecutive election [in 1990] to union leadership (by an overwhelming majority) was taken by the foreign press as support for his presidential aspirations.

After a series of statements in which they took potshots at one other, Wałęsa and Mazowiecki met on July 7. Instead of meeting at the shipyard, at "the source," as Wałęsa suggested, the two sides accepted an offer from Archbishop Bronisław Dąbrowski and met at one of the abbeys near Warsaw.[5] The subsequent press release contained nothing other than an announcement that the meeting took place (of course had they not said anything about further cooperation for the good of the country, it may

Lech Wałęsa declared that he would not speak French (photograph by Jerzy Gumowski, *Gazeta Wyborcza*).

have been taken as proof not only of a complete lack of understanding but of open political warfare).

The presidency was the main topic of discussion. But the six-hour conference did not bring the two closer in the least. Wałęsa left unwilling to make concessions on anything, banking on the other side's readiness to compromise. He was hoping to get a public affirmation of goodwill, but because of his stubbornness there could really be no discussion on this subject. And Wałęsa's stubbornness infected Mazowiecki, who would not budge either. Lech confirmed his desire to become president. He also tried to provoke Mazowiecki to take a stand on this subject. He succeeded. Mazowiecki confirmed what Wałęsa had been hearing for a long time from his closest advisors, something he did not wish to believe: that Mazowiecki would challenge him for the presidency. Wałęsa had first thought that Mazowiecki would not dare to make the bid. Then he imagined that Mazowiecki would back out during a face-to-face confrontation. It seems that Wałęsa thought that the presidential campaign would be a playoff at a rally where he could use his inborn abilities: reflexes, dynamism, self-assurance. These would play well against a plodding personality like Mazowiecki's. On July 8·the Solidarity trade commissions from the shipyards in the Tri-City (Gdańsk-Gdynia-Sopot) area called for a meeting with the Citizens' Parliamentary Caucus (OKP)[6] representatives at the Gdańsk shipyard. The discussion revealed that there had been a parting of the ways between Wałęsa and Mazowiecki.

The atmosphere at the July meeting at the shipyard workers' hall was very heavy. Wałęsa sat between the Kaczyński brothers. The room was brimming with workers. From under the huge Solidarity sign grave accusations were hurled at the government: The old (Communist) establishment is still in place; the government's power is concentrated in a small elite group; the economic policy of financial minister Leszek Balcerowicz is draconian; farming is unprofitable; the media is waging a campaign against Lech; capital is fleeing the country; the Communist order is solidifying; Małgorzata Niezabitowska, the Mazowiecki government's spokeswoman, is like Jerzy Urban, the old Communist government's press spokesman; the government is not "us" but "them"; the changes in the government are too small; there are too many taxes on income; production is falling; mining is a disaster; and so on.

Senators and OKP delegates, invited by the trade commissions of the various shipyards and ports in Gdańsk, took the podium in turn. They started their speeches by saying that they were not offended by the form of invitation (in essence they had been called on the carpet); they were expressing loyalty toward Lech and the pro–Center Alliance position.

Wałęsa got upset several times, cursing the dummies and dunderheads. He criticized the government and the so-called Left. He said that he would take the *Gazeta Wyborcza* to court. He spoke about the opportunities created by the self-dissolution of the PZPR and how they were being wasted. Members of shipyard Solidarity[7] reminded the representatives that it was thanks to them, the workers, that Solidarity started and reforms began. They demanded "a report from our representatives." In the minds of the port and shipyard avant-garde, the already dead idea of "the leadership of the working class" began to rejuvenate. Overall, Wałęsa was triumphant. The representatives who came for the most part shared his opinions. They talked about speeding things up, about the government-inspired apathy, the lost opportunities, Jaruzelski's expected resignation ...

During a break Lech met with a group of liberals—Janusz Lewandowski, Krzysztof Bielecki and others.[8] The conversation was short and to the point. The liberals stated their support for a Wałęsa candidacy. They felt that the reforms, especially in the economy, were going too slowly; that the Polish economy was "half-pregnant." Balcerowicz's ambitious austerity program, they believed, was hamstrung by Mazowiecki and parliament; the Left had too much influence. As the liberals saw it, Wałęsa, if he were president, could resolve this situation because many members of parliament were favorably inclined toward a Wałęsa presidency. Even the Communists would vote for Wałęsa in exchange for being allowed to back out of the political arena in a peaceful and dignified manner.

Wałęsa already knew from Jarosław Kaczyński about the results of the talks with Józef Czyrek, minister for international policy, and it looked like General Jaruzelski was ready to negotiate the conditions for his resignation. It seemed that Wałęsa was a step away from the desired end. The liberals pledged their total support in exchange for Wałęsa's support of their economic and legislative ideas, which also meant a number of political appointments. But there was one more condition: The change in leadership had to happen within the next few months (six at most). Because after that, most of them thought, Wałęsa the union leader will be seen as a revisionist and a populist candidate, an enemy of liberals. Wałęsa listened in silence. He grasped every word. After giving it some thought and despite his pronouncements in April, he answered, "Gentlemen, I must say no. It is too early. Our organization is not yet ready."

The liberals were decisive, realistic, and sure of themselves. They knew what they wanted. Lech, in contrast, gave the impression of being surprised by such a pragmatic conversation. He looked frightened. This was a feeling unknown to Wałęsa. Suddenly the presidency was a reality. Authority, and the responsibility that went with it, were within arm's reach. It was a totally new experience. During his battle with communism his authority as unofficial president was nearly limitless—but now the responsibility. Wałęsa was not ready for such an offer. Perhaps he sensed that the idea of being appointed by the parliament, while practical, was shoddy. He knew that after a few months he would have to stand a national election, most likely against Mazowiecki. It would be difficult to be able to point to any accomplishment after only a few months of governing. His instinct told him that he was being treated as an instrument. He refused but gained confidence in himself. It is possible that he thought that his election by the parliament was unlikely, and the specter of eventual defeat was too frightening. In July Lech decided to support the idea of popular elections for the presidency, a decision that came as quite a surprise to the Center Alliance.

On August 31, 1990, a hopeless attempt was made at mediation between the two most serious potential candidates for the office of president. On the tenth anniversary of the signing of the Gdańsk agreements that first confirmed Solidarity as an recognized labor union, the ways of the two politicians, Mazowiecki and Wałęsa, parted for good. The talks at the archbishop's residence were an attempt by one to convince the other to accept a different form of compromise. Wałęsa offered Mazowiecki a position as the head of the Council of Ministers—so that continuity of the executive could be maintained—in return for not contesting the presidency. Mazowiecki proposed that there be a third, independent candidate for president.

Mazowiecki, on the one hand, could not accept Wałęsa's proposal. It would be too hard for the prime minister willingly to give up his hard-won independence. It seemed that the prime minister was less optimistic about the union chief's chances than the chief himself. He was also aware that in such an alignment cooperation without conflicts would be impossible. Wałęsa, on the other hand, could not take the prime minister's proposal seriously. An independent candidate would not be able to handle the process of jump-starting the economic and political reforms. Lech decided that under these circumstances he was the only man who could help the nation.

On September 17, when Wałęsa formally announced his candidacy, he was moody and emotional. He repeated his short announcement, "I have decided," several times in front of the cameras. He did not make any further statements. The only other thing he did say to the gathered journalists was that this was a historic moment. He accepted Mazowiecki's candidacy without surprise but with some concern. "This candidacy," he said, "will complicate matters."

In trying to create an objective picture of Lech Wałęsa as president, I talked with some of his (present or former) close associates.

Jacek Merkel is a man who deals with realities. Ambitious, solid, a bear of a man, he builds confidence in others. He is a pragmatist. In any other country he would be a businessman. Merkel is Balcerowicz in a nicer wrapper. He is a fellow with a future. As he put it,

taking a position on the solid ground of formal logic and analyzing all the decisions made by Wałęsa, looking back ten years, I know that in the key situations, under difficult circumstances, he made the decisions. He himself. And those decisions were the correct ones. As it later proved, these were decisions that turned out to be beneficial for Poland. Very often he went against the experts or the activists. Let's look at the list.

August 1980: He was against the addition of the twenty-second postulate that would have introduced open elections for Sejm offices. It was a good postulate, but at the time it would have meant sure disaster. He also went against the idea of reforming the CRZZ [Central Council of Labor Unions],[9] which was championed by some of the experts. He found the golden center. He knew that we should ask for independent trade unions.

March 1981: The provocation in Bydgoszcz,[10] a general strike. Then the experts were very soft, while the activists wanted to go to the limits. He made the decision that we were not going to be pushed over the brink. He made it work by himself, against all others, even the entire KKP [National Commission of Understanding, the organ formed to lead and coordinate the Solidarity Union formed in 1980–1981], which later rightly accused him of exceeding his authority. He even manipulated one of the best-known activists—and said so himself: "I made a fool out of Andrzej Gwiazda."

On December 13, 1981, the government offered Wałęsa a chance to rebuild socialism. In this scenario Wałęsa was to play the leader of a "healthy worker's movement," while "extremist advisors" from KOR [Workers' Defense Committee] and KPN [Confederation of Independent Poland][11] were to be tossed out. Michnik told me that at the time he was convinced that Wałęsa would betray them. This is how they regarded him. After all, they warred with him for sixteen months, accusing him of being a Communist government security agent and other things. After some time had passed—at least he told it to me like this—Adam Michnik said, "We should treat Wałęsa to a half liter of vodka because he behaved like a man. He stood on principle. In a difficult moment he behaved as he should have and did not abandon us." Wałęsa, remembering those times, said, "I have led them out of the land of Egypt, the house of bondage."

At the Round Table[12] he was stubborn again. There is no freedom without Solidarity—this was the principle. The Communists had to choke out this slogan. Michnik and Kuroń had to sit at the Round Table. Geremek and Mazowiecki were ready to sell them out. It turned out that Wałęsa was right. The times were such that there had to be a united front.

Arkadiusz Rybicki, Wałęsa's secretary for many years: He raised the stakes in the negotiations. It threatened the entire undertaking for a while, but he had his reasons. He knew that if he gave in then he would be forced into further concessions. When he had the deciding voice, he picked the correct solutions.

Jacek Merkel: When I see so many meaningful moments, I am led to believe that this man can get a handle on it, and he will be able to manage.

Aleksander Hall: Lech, as president, has too many gaps in his competence. He could compensate, if he had a greater ability for listening. After all, a president does not have to be an expert on everything. But Lech lost this ability. Wałęsa thinks that he knows better by using his nose for guidance. No doubt for a politician a nose is an ultraimportant item, but I would like to add that by itself it is inadequate. Lech cannot place himself within the rules that govern a democratic country. That which a union leader could get away with, especially in a union that had been driven underground, will not pass when he is president. The road Lech has chosen in his march to the presidency is bad for Poland, and, most important, it is bad for him. The myth of Wałęsa that united all and made some see him as a symbol, others see him as an inspired leader, and made all regard him as a national legend, is over. I disagree with Michnik's categorical statement that the Wałęsa presidency will be a disaster. Lech has his virtues; he is politically agile and no doubt is an exceptional person. I can see chances, albeit small, that Lech will again surprise us.

Arkadiusz Rybicki: Wałęsa has many negative attributes, and public opinion [in October 1990] is concentrating on these. But he has positive ones as well. I admire him for the absolute faith he has in the things he does. This is not a common virtue among politicians.

Wałęsa is disciplined. Many people in the government camp are used to the opposition-journalist life-style, where one talks until midnight, drinks vodka, coffee, tea, and then sleeps until 10 a.m. just to get by. These habits are impossible to overcome. Lech is different.

Wojciech Jaruzelski, Lech Wałęsa, and Bronisław Geremek on the front bench in parliament (photograph by Sławomir Sierzputowski, *Gazeta Wyborcza*).

Wałęsa does not like talk. The awful, repetitive babbling is the bane of political life. Everyone must have a say. Everybody is very important and must get a sacred version of the truth out. This can be seen in the Sejm. But it is really unnecessary. It is a question of the idea and the decision.

Wałęsa is very mobile. He can be in several places at once and still have time for his family.

I am sure that he has a feel for being the Polish head of state. Wałęsa can offer cooperation to his opponents. This is one of his virtues. When he becomes president he will offer important appointments to his opponents. In this way he will reconcile with those people and make them part of his policy. He will eliminate them as the opposition. It is a fact that he has no political vision. This is a major fault. But in Poland not one political vision has ever proved out. Someone like [Mikhail] Gorbachev was not foreseen by the intellectuals. It could be said that the things that have happened in Europe during the last two years have, in a sense, compromised the intellectuals.

The president will not be the only ruling force in Poland. There will be other parallel centers of power. The church will keep its position. There will be parliament. There will be political parties. He will have some very strong opposition. He will come into office in a very weakened state. His opponents will be the spearhead of the Polish political movement: Mazowiecki, Hall, Michnik. That is why Wałęsa's hands will be tied. Of course there is still the possible scenario of what will happen if protests, street violence, and riots break out.

Adam Michnik: I think that the president should guarantee the continuity of political thought that started with prime minister Mazowiecki. That is the philosophy of evolutionary change, without force, without creating new political conflicts. The president must be believable in the public mind, here and abroad. He should be a mediator in the conflicts that arise among various centers of power. Therefore he may not be one who is unpredictable, unaccountable, irresponsible, self-important, and lacking competence. If he is a predictable politician, then it means that his program and future actions will not be a guessing game or a coin toss—this is unallowable even when the president is a person of incredible talent. He must be responsible for his words and gestures. This means that he cannot say one thing in the morning, another in the afternoon, and then hold a grudge against the reporters for twisting his words around. He must be self-effacing, that is, a politician who does not sing his own praises, who does not think that all the good ideas were his because it goes with the authority of his office. And at last a competent politician, one who knows the importance of information but not competent in the sense that he knows everything—since there is no such man—but in the sense that he knows what he does not know and then manages to avoid ignorant comments about economics or international relations, remarks that are frightening.

The second question concerns the concept of the president's office. I would like to have a normal president in a normal nation of laws. I would not want to have a president whose position would be special, like that held by Napoleon Bonaparte before he declared himself emperor. I would not want someone who would occupy this office as a Flying Dutchman who would roam around Poland with an ax, hunting down the [Communist] establishment; tracking down thieves, confiscating newspapers; giving out millions; and being a whole lot more than a president. He would be an uncrowned monarch.

What was a major virtue for Wałęsa during the twenty-year career in the opposition has become an unallowable liability in the new times, which need stability, respect for law, and the rebuilding of authority (not partisanship).

Journalist Piotr Wierzbicki, in the February 9, 1990, issue of *Tygodnik Solidarność* (Solidarity weekly),[13] was enthusiastic about one such quality:

> Hurrah, bravo, long live unpredictable Wałęsa! Someone like him is necessary to all Poles. Here's a man who can act unpredictably; his opponents cannot hope to get the measure of him. Unpredictability is the major political virtue. Unpredictability is a method for winning battles and wars. Doesn't one become the victorious chieftain by acting in unpredictable ways? Wasn't the weakest quality of the underground Solidarity movement its predictability of action? They announced their plan for observing the anniversaries of various events so that the ZOMO [riot police] knew where and when to wait for the demonstrators. They were open and honestly straight with their opponents. May unpredictable Wałęsa counteract this unfortunate predictability.

But in a democratic Poland there is no ZOMO, and it is possible to negotiate with the opposition (if it must exist). Unpredictable Wałęsa could not manage to negotiate during the time Mazowiecki was in office. Unpredictability is not a presidential virtue.

Wałęsa was the unofficial president of Poland: He could create a coalition, appoint a prime minister, call for participation in elections. He had power and yet was not saddled with constitutional responsibility. His awareness of the responsibility for the effects of his policies could have a calming and quieting effect. It could happen that he would listen to advice more eagerly, a trait that up to now was not among his strong points. And one could not eliminate the possibility that Wałęsa would surprise everyone in a positive way and say, "And you see, I was right after all!"

* * *

An interviewer asked, "Did you know that the largest conference room at the Belweder Palace can hold only 100 persons, and it looks as if the large National Commission could never meet there?" Lech Wałęsa answered, "Then we will sit on each other's lap with three people to a chair."

— *Tygodnik Solidarność*, April 27, 1990

In this political situation, under which pluralism has advanced far, I will try to create order, but without malice. But the people will think it malicious. Others will try to make a sensation of it.

—Lech Wałęsa, June 5, 1990, Warsaw

The Citizens' Committee under the Solidarity chief was established on December 18, 1988. It gathered the Polish anti-Communist elite from all levels—intellectuals, scholars, writers, lawyers, actors, and opposition activists. The intention of its creators, people who had for a long time formed the democratic opposition to the regime, mainly in the KOR organization, was to make it an expression of their own expectations and longings. The committee would make statements and formulate political positions in the face of the Communist regime. It was going to be a moral force and an instrument for applying political pressure to the Polish government. Many of its members had represented Solidarity in the Round Table negotiations. While Wałęsa, by unanimous consent, was the committee's titular patron, there was no formal leader who would oversee the day-to-day functioning of the committee.

That is why the nomination of Zdzisław Najder in the middle of March 1990 for the leadership of the Citizens' Committee under Lech Wałęsa caused a great deal of consternation in Warsaw. The action was perceived as an unequivocal affront by Lech against Geremek and the people in the presidium of the OKP who were the founders of the Citizens' Committee. (It is worthwhile to remember that the committee added "under Lech Wałęsa" to its name only on October 27, 1990. Before then, its title had been the Citizens' Committee Under the Chairman of the Solidarity Labor Union.) Wałęsa felt that he was losing control over the things connected with his name to—as he put it—"the left leg."[1] Geremek answered with noble silence.

Instead of a reply from Geremek, Adam Michnik arrived in Gdańsk. Adam thought that Najder was a man of ideas, of crystal honesty, ready to do great deeds, but that he had one great political flaw: his contentiousness. "He could not work with people; he created misunderstandings and intrigues. After all, his history at Radio Free Europe, where he was a director, should give you something to think about." Michnik tried to explain the facts to Wałęsa. "Indeed the loss of his directorship resulted not from the quality of his work but because of his difficult manner. You are risking the breakup of the committee. The people will not want to work with him."

Lech reacted in a lively manner. The conversation resembled one between a blind man on the one side and a deaf one on the other. Lech started to insert frequent anecdotes that were only partly funny; then he switched to double entendres. He made allusions to a conspiracy, mafia-like tendencies, something about the Left and the socialists, some dirt being done, and so on. He blamed Michnik for having the PZPR split into two, not three parts, as he supposedly had planned. This scenario was to have happened as a result of Michnik's television debates with Aleksander Kwaśniewski. "Lech, I don't understand you," answered Michnik, "but I'd like you to know that I leave here in the same state of confusion in which I came."

Michnik left more shocked than disappointed. He could not comprehend how the Communist party was to have split into three parts and why it was fine for Wałęsa to meet with Mieczysław Rakowski, a top Communist, but bad for Michnik to meet with Kwaśniewski. After that meeting I was tortured by the question why people who have worked together for years can so completely confuse each other by using language neither understands.

Wałęsa listened to many, deftly maneuvering among opinions. He was suspicious of everyone. But he liked Michnik very much; he was deferential to him, valued his directness, and respected his intelligence. Michnik himself stated his unshakable loyalty to Lech. His loyalty was not toppled by this unfortunate conversation. The real break in their relationship came when Lech wrote a letter of dismissal to Michnik, relieving him as editor and taking away the Solidarity logo from *Gazeta Wyborcza*.[2]

Michnik is a passionate man whose emotions run deep or not at all. With the letter of dismissal, he went from extreme loyalty to utter lack of faith.

But two weeks after Michnik's visit in Gdańsk, after the March 17 meeting with Havel, Michnik still believed in Wałęsa. We were leaving by helicopter, flying to Sosnowiec—Wałęsa to a rally, Michnik to a meeting of Sejm deputies. The noise was horrendous. Lech put on headphones, settled into a seat, and tried to sleep.

Michnik and I sat in neighboring seats. To communicate we had to shout. Lech could hear everything we had to say. We were drinking brandy from a Kodak film container.

Lech Wałęsa stated that *Gazeta Wyborcza* could no longer use the Solidarity logo (photograph by Krzysztof Miller, *Gazeta Wyborcza*).

I thought that loyalty to one's chief also requires one to tell him unpleasant things. That is why chiefs are lonely people.

Few have the courage to speak the absolute truth. In Wałęsa's group they were scarce indeed. But those who can do it are often wasting their effort, because Lech is not a grateful listener. He is incredibly stubborn. I decided to relate to him my conversation with Michnik. I had warned Michnik beforehand; he had no objections.

Two persons with widely differing perspectives, that is, Adam Michnik and Leszek Kaczyński, came to the same conclusion: that our chief makes too many appearances talking too much about trivial matters and that he should tone it down. Lech would not listen to any advice on this subject.

Michnik said that Wałęsa should move slowly but deliberately because the last few months were a running mistake. The weekly press conferences were nonsense, a waste of political resources before Wałęsa's ascent to the presidency (in Michnik's mind this was not a question of if but when).

Michnik thought that the later Wałęsa became president the better. It took France, Italy, and Germany from eight to twelve years to lick their wounds after World War II. They did not change their political systems but went to work on their economies with the benefit of the Marshall Plan. The Polish way of doing things would take only five years—at least according to the optimistc forecast of Balcerowicz, the finance minister. Michnik thought that we would start to run out of steam after a year, sometime around April or May 1991. Then it would have to be Wałęsa who would occupy the presidential chair. Up to that time we would have to preserve Jaruzelski because he is a politician with no future, one who paradoxically guarantees the post–Round Table alignment and peace for Balcerowicz to introduce his reforms.

We agreed that Wałęsa would be a president who not only utilized his constitutional authority to the fullest but often stretched it past the limits. Dissolution of the Sejm, changes in government and in prime ministers, would become the future daily order of Polish political life, which has the activities of Piłsudski after 1926 as its model.[3] It must be remembered, however, that Wałęsa is not Piłsudski and that post-Communist Poland is not the prewar second Polish republic.

On March 31 a meeting with the Citizens' Committee was to take place. When we arrived, together with the government bodyguards, at 54 Polanki Street, Lech was not in front of his house. "The exercise yard is empty," announced one of the bodyguards.

Wałęsa is extremely punctual, can't stand to be late, and so usually waits for the car on the fenced, concrete area in front of the house. This space, with its tall fence, resembles a prison exercise yard. The term, used by Wałęsa and his bodyguards, bore testimony to the sense of imprisonment the chief now felt. A few months earlier, when Wałęsa's permanent bodyguards (assigned by someone in Warsaw) arrived, Janusz Palubicki, a member of the KKW presidium, almost fainted on entering Lech's office. He returned to the conference room white as a sheet and said, "At the door of Wałęsa's office sits a guy who was my personal guard when I was arrested. He sat by my bed in the hospital like a brick wall." During a break in the discussion each member of the group, using some facile pretext, ran over to the chief's office to get a good look at this specimen.

The gate squeaked; then we were on our way. Wałęsa knew that he was going to endure a difficult ordeal.

He had nominated Najder to head the steering group of the Citizens' Committee; now he had to legitimize the appointment. Najder was part of the Polish Independence Alliance, an opposition group from the 1970s that brought together various intellectual leaders. One of its activists was Olszewski, a lawyer who became Najder's right hand in his work with the committee. The organization had the support of Tadeusz Mazowiecki. The old political ties between Mazowiecki and Najder took on a personal coloring because even during the time of the Round Table discussions, Mazowiecki forcefully tried to convince (the Communist) minister

Czesław Kiszczak to "rehabilitate" his friend, who had been given the death sentence in absentia by the Communist government.

The members of the Citizens' Committee (Geremek, the moving spirit of the committee, was in the United States at the time of the meeting; Michnik was absent as well) would not want to recognize Najder, an outsider, as their chairman. After all, the committee had been formed by a group of activists from the old KOR who had put the bulk of their political effort into its creation and activities. Lech knew this well. But he maintained that no institution, no instrument, should stay in the hands of one politician for too long, otherwise it would lead to an undemocratic situation.

Najder's nomination was typical of Wałęsa actions and analogous to his nomination of Mazowiecki as prime minister. Both moves were unpredictable, surprising everyone, including the persons in question; neither nominee was associated with the Left, and at the time of nomination each man was in a political backwater. Because of his long absence from Poland, Najder was not politically aligned with any camp and openly declared his loyalty to Lech. His nomination caused a storm of protest, which only pushed him closer to Wałęsa, his natural ally.

During a March 14, 1990, interview given to *Głos Wielkopolski* (Voice of Wielkopolska)[4] Wałęsa gave the following explanation for the changes in his team:

> I did it in an entirely democratic manner. That is why I appointed Najder, who was an unbeaten man—or perhaps a man beaten by all sides, which also has the effect that he stands straight—so that the Citizens' Parliamentary Caucus would have its part to play and not turn into a monopoly. I appointed him so that the Citizens' Parliamentary Caucus would not impose its will on others but remain only one of the factors. Of course, Lech Wałęsa belongs to the Citizens' Parliamentary Caucus, which is an alliance of all other viewpoints that, on the principles of peace, pluralism, honesty, want to participate and have something to say. I want to make possible a place for them in the elections, in the programs, in all that we do today. That is why I will not give control of the Citizens' Committee to the OKP.

On June 1 Lech arrived at work in a good mood. He asked me into his office and dictated the outline of a letter to Wujec, the secretary of the Citizens' Committee. Wujec is modest and unpretentious. He takes great words and turns them into real deeds; he is as mobile and industrious as an ant. (If every Pole were like Wujec, we would be another Japan.) I remember this day well. I knew it would negatively affect Lech's prestige. He was dictating nothing less than Wujec's letter of dismissal.

Henryk!

The elections are over, so this is a good time to make several necessary changes in the organization of the committee. As you know, in my own vision the Citizens' Committee should have a broader political formula. It cannot be part of the government's or the OKP's infrastructure.

This point of view forced me to make the painful decision to relieve you of the position of secretary. What makes this difficult for me to do is that I am aware of the valuable work you have done there. I trust that as a politician you will understand my motivation and the necessity for this decision.

I would like you to hand all matters over to Zdzisław Najder.

I would, once more, like to thank you for your selfless effort and wish you the best of luck in your continuing work in the cause of Poland.

Lech Wałęsa, June 1, 1990.

Wałęsa must have had the change in mind for some time. He would not allow anyone to advise him on it. "We must clear this up," he said.

We did not yet have an answer from Wujec when Wałęsa again asked me into his office. I was to take down a second letter of dismissal. This time it was for Adam Michnik. The text was as follows:

Adam!

As we are friends working together, it will not be difficult to resolve the problems that have arisen in reference to your newspaper. I see two necessities:

1. I must dismiss you as the head editor of *Gazeta Wyborcza* (since I appointed you I believe that I can dismiss you).

2. I must take away the right of *Gazeta Wyborcza* to use the Solidarity logo.

Because I am forced to undertake this course of action, and would like to do it as befits friends, please tell me the form this should take.

Lech Wałęsa, June 1, 1990.

And again appeals were to no avail. Pusz and I were talking at him, "Lech, you will make a laughing stock of yourself. The *Gazeta Wyborcza* is published by a corporation. It is edited by a team of editors—not by you. You cannot dismiss Michnik; you simply don't have the authority. Phone him yourself. Talk to him, since you call him a friend. Lech, a letter like this will do you a lot of harm. It is a suicidal shot."

He had one answer: "Fax this to Michnik immediately." Wałęsa stood over me. He was looking at my hands, accusing me of sluggishness. The letter was like a court sentence.

Michnik was not in the editorial office. Wałęsa then ordered Krzysztof to relay the letter by telephone. Krzysztof did it that evening. Michnik was speechless. After a moment he concluded that he should accept

Jarosław Kaczyński and Lech Wałęsa during a lull in the action (photograph by Tomasz Wierzejski, *Gazeta Wyborcza*).

Wałęsa's decision and resign. He delivered his resignation at the next meeting of the editorial team. But the resignation was not accepted.

The chief went home in a good mood. A moment later an answer arrived from Wujec.

> Dear Lech!
> Thank you for the greetings. It appears that due to overwork you have forgotten that my appointment as secretary of the Citizens' Committee Under the Chairman of the Solidarity Labor Union was the result of an election in the Citizens' Committee and only the committee has the authority to remove me.
> Of course I am ready to resign all my duties at the moment that the Citizens' Committee asks for my resignation.
> Warsaw, June 1, 1990.

I called Wałęsa and read the letter. There was a dead silence in the receiver.

"Write 'Consider yourself dismissed.'"

"Is that all?" I asked.

"Yes. Send it immediately."

I sent it.

Before he left for home, Lech sat at his desk and pulled a pile of papers from his briefcase. He picked out one page, a statement condemning anti-Semitism. The pretext for issuing this was to be the approaching forty-fourth anniversary of a Jewish pogrom in Kielce. The proclamation began: "In one month, the 44th anniversary will pass." I asked myself, if the anniversary is a month away (on July 4) why is Lech so anxious to release this statement now? Could it be to head off accusations that Michnik's dismissal is an act of anti-Semitism? Hell, who wrote this for him? Who is inciting him to start a media circus? I thought out loud—Najder.

"Najder wrote this for you!"

"No," Wałęsa answered, looking me straight in the eye.

I did not believe him.

Yet the real author had to be either Najder or Leszek Kaczyński. I decided to check it out. But Kaczyński's eyes bugged out when he heard about the dismissal of Wujec, though he thought the move was correct. He expected, however, that Lech would do it in a more democratic manner, during the committee's meeting on June 24. It was at a social gathering, and quite by accident, that he learned about the attempt to dismiss Michnik.

Everything was falling into its logical place. This was a carefully laid plan and Lech was its executor. First Lech dismisses Wujec, who was a thorn in Najder's side because as the secretary of the Citizens' Committee he denied Najder, whom Wałęsa nominated, any real power. For Wałęsa, Wujec was a symbol of the link between the Citizens' Committee, the Solidarity Left, and the presidium of the OKP. Najder himself explained the matter to the BBC:

> *Najder:* In the committee, the leadership was split between the secretariat and myself as chairman. I think that this had a bad effect on the work of the whole. Besides this, there is really nothing to say.
>
> *BBC:* Then this means that the Solidarity chairman [Wałęsa] did not consult with you on this matter?
>
> *Najder:* Dear sir, the chairman never concealed his intention to separate the institutions of the Citizens' Committee and the Citizens' Parliamentary Caucus. Our personal liaison was Henryk Wujec as secretary of both groups, and he did not hide before me his own worry over the fact that conflicts were arising over who is responsible for what. I was the titular chairman, but outside of calling the meetings to order and sending out notices I had no real power, while Mr. Wujec handled not only the contacts with committees in the field, because we agreed to this, but all the matters that I wished to handle. It was an unhealthy situation, and I could not hide it from the chairman.

On Monday, June 4, Wałęsa released a long statement explaining the need for personnel and organizational changes in the committee. The text was written in the same style, with the same typewriter, and on the same paper as was the Kielce statement.

Most painful, for me, was not so much the confirmation that Najder was the instigator of this affair but the knowledge that Lech acted on his suggestions without analyzing their effect. Wałęsa, concluding that the presidium of the OKP was "in league with the government," decided to act. Any action against them seemed good. Wałęsa, who always used his intuition to pick the most appropriate course of action, started to act chaotically. In accordance with the radical ideas belonging to the Chairman of the Citizens' Committee, he became the hatchet man. The Kaczyński brothers were his dumbfounded audience. Because the chief's moves were too radical (even though they were along the lines of policy the brothers promulgated), Leszek joined in the attempts to change Wałęsa's mind. We could only make him agree to change the text. The fruit of our mediation was the following letter:

> Adam!
>
> Before the elections on June 4, 1989, I appointed you to the position of head editor at the *Gazeta Wyborcza*. Time has moved on and in between a corporation was formed under the name "Agora," which then became the publisher of your paper. In this situation my appointment is really without basis. You should seek a new appointment from the corporation.
>
> We should also consider whether a publication issued by a private corporation should have the further use of the Solidarity logo.
>
> Lech Wałęsa, June 4, 1990

The close cooperation between the Kaczyński brothers and Wałęsa has affected public perceptions in such a way that the brothers bear all responsibility only for the chief's unpopular actions: All that is good is initiated by the chief; all that is bad is the fault of his associates, mainly the Kaczyński brothers.

On June 7th Wałęsa himself informed me about the sins ascribed to my account. On the previous day the Reuters news agency, and after them the other Western media, printed the text of the Michnik-Wałęsa correspondence. Since the news was already public, Michnik felt released from the obligation of keeping things under wraps. That very morning an issue of *Gazeta Wyborcza*, with the full text of the correspondence on the front page, landed on Lech's desk. Michnik wrote: "Neither I nor any of my associates at *Gazeta Wyborcza* released any of this information to the mass media."

Wałęsa threw a fit. Because only he, Kaczyński, Pusz, and I knew the content of the letters, Lech deduced that I had leaked them. The supposed proof was my passivity toward Michnik's defamatory statements. (Wałęsa accused me of being Michnik's protector, of being in league with him, manipulated by Michnik and Geremek.) I was faced with a false assertion that I had behaved dishonestly. Lech was very unpleasant. He yelled and waved his finger in front of my face. The upshot of all this talk was that the affair was completely my fault.

"Why did you not find the guilty party?"

"Because my job is to give out information, not to conduct investigations," I answered.

"You have seen how Michnik lies about me, and you do nothing. Write a statement immediately, or you're fired."

"You can fire me; I'm ready to go anytime."

"I'll have to think about it," he murmured.

The tension decreased. In my statement I wrote that on Wałęsa's direction I faxed the letters to a number given to me by Michnik. I gave the letters to no one else. I added that since Reuters was the first press agency to release the content of the letters, and its correspondent resides in Warsaw, he must have learned about them from someone in that city. For Wałęsa this was not enough. He expected me to attack Michnik, calling him a liar and a dissembler. I told him to get himself a director of propaganda. "This isn't any good. Something like this is not worth publishing," said Wałęsa.

Adam, a man who trusts his people, held to the belief that no one in the editorial office had leaked the information. (I later learned from Reuters that their man at *Gazeta Wyborcza* gave them the information.) And Lech purposely moved the matter of the leaked correspondence to center stage, masking the true issue of the dismissal.

I met Wałęsa two hours later at the weekly press conference, which on this occasion was given at the Gdańsk Medical Academy. There was a large audience in the auditorium, a mix of everyone from nurses to professors of medicine. Lech did not miss the opportunity to suggest that it was I who had leaked the text of the private correspondence. I was ready for this. I read the previously cited statement, which Lech dismissed as meaningless. It was one of the most difficult moments of our working relationship. He knew that he was teaching me a lesson in public. I did not want to start an open conflict.

At the conference he was in an excellent mood. He was in his element. He threw out some jokes and used concise metaphors easily understood by the crowd. As always he spoke in a way so as not to polarize his audience. Because each sentence was contrary to the next, listeners tried to grab the general content of the speech. Each person did it on an indi-

vidual basis, connecting personal wishes and thoughts to the general pronouncements. Sitting next to him, I felt the tremendous power contained
in this man. The frightening thing was that Lech was able to deal so easily
with a crowd composed of so many different individual personalities. I
felt that anyone who would stand against Lech would lose, be defeated,
crushed.

The press conference was almost a forewarning of a new movement—
a movement calling for a "moral cleansing." At the head of this
movement would stand a leader endowed with the public trust, who in
the name of his own interests—which would be one and the same with
those of Poland—would create a political power to promulgate second-
rate ideals. Wałęsa is capable of setting loose forces that no one can
control. He can awaken phobias, solidify embryonic divisions. It is unfortunate that the current economic crisis of unfathomable dimensions
favors movements that use the rhetoric of radical, immediate change. The
crisis also favors the creation of strong, decisive leaders. Wałęsa is an
example of a leader who is extremely well qualified because the people
can put trust in him to a large degree as the person who toppled
communism and who loves freedom, having risked his own neck for it.

Testifying to the quality of the concepts propagated by Lech would be
his supporters, his political allies. On this list the very first names would
belong to those who have passed for his opponents. Like a ship, Lech
gathers all sorts of unclean barnacles—the rotten remnants of the Polish
political scene. At the conference in the Gdańsk Medical Academy,
Wałęsa awakened the enthusiasm of the lower and middle echelons and
gained the sympathies of the intellectual elite. But still, one of the young
surgeons accused him of thoughtless acts that were spoiling the efforts of
the emergency rescue team trying to restore Poland to health. A similar
theme was present in Michnik's June 4 reply to Wałęsa's letter:

> Lech!
> You know well that I have always talked with you openly. It will be so
> this time. Time has progressed further than it would seem from your letter.
> From the leader of Solidarity, the mass movement of Polish democracy,
> you are slowly turning into Cæsar who in turn sends his friends instruc-
> tions: "Consider yourself dismissed." Your letter to Henryk Wujec I see not
> only as a political mistake but as a moral error. I am asking you, as a friend,
> to reverse this bad and unwise decision. Your pronouncements "I am
> ashamed of the government" are harmful to Poland. Take some time to
> consider how you would feel if I spoke like this about a government you
> led.
> I share your view that the editor in chief of *Gazeta Wyborcza* should be
> chosen by the corporation, not by the chairman of the Solidarity labor

union. After receiving your letter I handed in my resignation to my colleagues, but it was not accepted.

Naturally, I am ready to discuss with you all the matters that are important to Poland—as we have done before. You know well why for ten years I have been loyal to the Solidarity logo. I believe that I have never disgraced it.

Adam Michnik, June 4, 1990

The exchange of correspondence between Wałęsa and Wujec and Michnik delighted those few who considered these moves proper—and the journalists who started to call my office. They wanted to know the reasons for Wałęsa's actions and the future plans the chief had, that is, who was next on the list. I answered tersely; the whole affair was embarrassing to me.

The journalists had something to write about. Wałęsa's mysterious moves were beginning to coalesce into a rather dark whole. The "war" Wałęsa announced finally broke out. The lines of battle had formed; there were even casualties. Wujec was hit and went down, then Michnik, gravely wounded. Wałęsa himself was not without losses in men and equipment. One could speculate who was going to get it next and where the commands were coming from. The foreign correspondents were overjoyed that their stories from Poland were making it to the front pages under interesting headlines like "Wałęsa's Head is Spinning" (*L'Express*, June 22, 1990), "Solidarity's Solid Front Crumbles from Within: Rout of Common Foe Perils Common Cause" (*Washington Post*, June 6, 1990), "Politics Are Coming to the Foreground—But the Poles Are Unaware" (*Le Monde*, June 6, 1990).

On June 1, the day the whole affair with Wujec burst out into the open, I submitted to the Norwegian committee for the Nobel Peace Prize a nomination from Lech Wałęsa, the 1983 recipient of the award. It named the peoples of Lithuania, Latvia, and Estonia as worthy of the prize. Normally this would have been the big news. On Friday it drowned in a flood of speculation about the Wałęsa's personnel changes.

On June 3 Lech's name-day celebration[5] was to be another chance for reconciliation. But Geremek was the only one to show up from the crowd who usually came from Warsaw for such events. He said that the reason for his coming was to demonstrate personally that the separation between Gdańsk and Warsaw was not final.

The host was in a good mood; he poured champagne for the guests and encouraged them to join in the feast. In spite of protests, he did take a half hour to have a conversation with Geremek in the garden, after which both seemed satisfied. Geremek even said publicly that he was leaving with an optimistic viewpoint. But in truth he left depressed.

Leszek Kaczyński spent the entire evening and part of the next day trying to figure out the cause for Geremek's optimism after the conversation with Lech. By then it was clear that the planned Monday meeting, which was to be devoted to turning Lech away from "political maneuvering," would not take place. It was rescheduled at the request of prime minister Mazowiecki, who said that he wanted to take part in the meeting but would not be able to do so on the day slated. A few days later Pusz forced the real reason out of Jacek Ambroziak, chief of the council of ministers, who admitted that the date was changed for reasons of prestige.

The day after the party, Lech spoke favorably of Geremek saying, "He was the only one who did not go against me." Indeed, the professor still lived the myth of August 1980, the time he and Mazowiecki brought to the strikers in Gdańsk a letter of support signed by sixty-four intellectuals. Although the strike committee was against having them remain at the shipyard, Wałęsa named them as advisors and forced consent of the others. For Geremek, this was an important experience. His history in the opposition is not as long and rich as that of Kuroń, Michnik, or Mazowiecki. Geremek's political activities were centered mainly on the Solidarity movement and, until recently, on the person who symbolizes that movement, Lech Wałęsa. Geremek had (and I admit that he still may have) Wałęsa's great respect. Wałęsa knows that the professor is a partner, an important figure—a lieutenant.

Geremek is a master of political technique, who can wait to the last moment before making the decisive move. He is multilingual, erudite, aware of his own worth, extremely cultured. When we flew to the Karkonosze Mountains to meet Havel, Geremek talked with Wałęsa. This was the time when political alignments were beginning to shift. There was much to discuss. But the conversation would not flow, instead resembling a session in the office of an experienced psychoanalyst. Wałęsa, unable to cope with Geremek's arguments, tried to turn the conversation to humor or trivia. He switched from topic to topic, talking about things that could fill a book of political absurdities. Geremek knew when to laugh, when to be serious, when to mock Wałęsa by saying "Mr. Chairman appears to have eaten of the locoweed!" Few can permit themselves similar familiarities. Geremek's harsh criticism often took a masked form difficult for Lech to recognize. But he knew it was there. Even so he treated the professor with great respect. Geremek knows what to say and to whom to say it in order to get the necessary effect. His corrections to the text of the press release at the Wałęsa-Havel meeting were done with tact and grace.

In the Sejm at the end of January, during the conference of the citizens' committees that was devoted to the Solidarity movement,[6] the professor felt alienated. As was seen later, he correctly anticipated a move by Jarosław Kaczyński calculated to block the formation of a political party on the foundation of the citizens' committees. Such a party would have had the spirit of Solidarity as its ideological basis and committees across Poland.

Geremek's nerve failed him when he had to go head-to-head with Kaczyński. As he presided over the meeting, it was his function to assure order. Although the speakers were not limited to a certain time, it was his duty to speed up lengthy pronouncements by tapping the edge of a glass with a spoon. Kaczyński barely got started when the glass tinkled. Part of the audience broke into laughter.

In the final phase of the Geremek-Wałęsa alliance, the professor limited himself to faxing Lech items about Wałęsa that appeared in the Western press, adding a handwritten notation along the lines of "Pleasant reading." During the June meeting of the Citizens' Committee, he asked rhetorically, without hiding his bitterness, "Is today's Lech Wałęsa the man whom I knew for years? If Lech has changed, then I feel like a man who is not of this century." The last time I saw Geremek talking with Wałęsa was on June 29, 1990, at a Vienna meeting devoted to East European matters. Wałęsa harangued nervously. Geremek answered, "Lech, more distance please, more distance!"

On June 5 Lech took off on a special government plane in the company of Bishop Gocłowski, secretary of state Nowina-Konopka, Pusz, and myself. Our destination was Warsaw and a meeting with the Vatican secretary of state, Agostino Casaroli. Just before departure Wałęsa gave an interview to Maria Mrozinska of *Gazeta Gdańska* in which he explained the motivation for his actions in respect to Wujec and Michnik. He concluded that he had trusted his friends and associates too far in that they blocked his initiatives so that he could not get anything done. "I can't do anything in the Solidarity Foundation.[7] I can't change the committee's secretary. Supposedly the committee is under me, but I have no say-so."

We took off. With a large kitchen knife Lech started opening a pile of envelopes stacked before him. "I believed in my friends—Jews—and they made a fool out of me," he said. "I was warned many times not to get involved with Jews, that I should not get into their circle and take their advice. I always answered that these were my friends, colleagues. So what happens? They worked me over! Now I won't let them manipulate me."

The entire trip from Gdańsk to Warsaw, over an hour, was one incredible harangue in which everyone, Bishop Gocłowski included, tried to convince Lech that a catastrophe would result from his using this kind of argument (not to mention its moral implications). Wałęsa was amused by the terror his words inspired among his traveling companions. His pretense that he believed in what he was saying was very convincing. (He was so convincing, in fact, that I could no longer tell where this absurd game ended and reality began.) He was having a wonderful time. We were not amused.

After landing we proceeded to the nuncio's residence. If not for Pusz, who said that Wałęsa was putting on an act, I would have been firmly convinced that Wałęsa was going to add anti-Semitic references to his political repertoire. I had told him that anti-Semitic statements would cause his political downfall, would finish him as a politician and as a man. This did not happen. The journalists asking Lech about the affair with Michnik and Wujec never heard any of the statements made ten minutes earlier on the plane.

On July 4 the Solidarity foreign bureau received a telex with a message from the Holocaust Memorial Institute Yad Vashem in Israel "The governing body of Yad Vashem has expressed grave concern in reference to the statements about Jews in the political and party disputes in the countries of Eastern Europe. Especially troubling are the statements made by the leader of Solidarity, Lech Wałęsa, which were published by the media. Statements of this nature, even if unintentional, can reinforce anti-Semitic feelings." A few weeks later, in August, Western readers were informed that Lech Wałęsa said that he did not understand why the Jews in the Polish government and parliament are trying to hide their ethnicity.

This and several other statements were among the reasons Schewach Weiss, the vice-marshal of the Israeli parliament, the Knesset, made the trip to Gdańsk at the beginning of September. His meeting with Wałęsa lasted over an hour. Afterwards Weiss announced that he was satisfied with the assurances Wałęsa gave to the effect that the unfortunate statements were a misunderstanding. He also accepted Wałęsa's declaration of friendship for the Jewish people. Wałęsa told Weiss that he would never allow any form of anti-Semitism in Poland. He added, "I have proved that I am not an anti-Semite. I say this openly to the world, Poland, and the Jewish people." Weiss in an aside said, "We came here to find out how things really stand. We gave him a chance. Since he said that he is not anti-Semitic, then we have no reason to doubt it."

The effect was instantaneous. On September 14 the Israeli minister of religion, Avner Shaky, relayed a letter to Wałęsa through the Polish legation in Israel: "I would like to offer my thanks and the thanks of many other Israeli people to the great leader of Poland for his unequivocal statement and the brave stand he took against the reawakening of anti-Semitism in his own country and everywhere else. Anti-Semitism is one of the most offensive forms of racism, and all opponents of racism should speak out against it."

At a press conference on September 13, Wałęsa himself tried to explain why he was being accused of anti-Semitism.

For a long time I did not know how I got mixed up with the subject of anti-Semitism. After all, ladies and gentlemen, I was doing all I could so that there would be no place for anti-Semitism in Poland. I have proof of this. I have nothing in common with Jews, I am not a Jew, there are no Jews in my family, but I am not anti-Semitic. But somehow I was being mixed up with these things which left me thinking how this came about. Well, you see, I have been elevated to this position by the people; I am one of them. People ask all sorts of questions. There are many questions; some of them are absurd; rarely are they anti-Semitic. But there are questions like, "Is so and so a Jew?" or "Are there not too many Jews in the government?" These questions are submitted. I try to address these questions, so the very fact that I deal with this problem suggests that I may be anti-Semitic. ... This is how sensitive people can be on this subject. My approach to this matter is as follows. Why should a man be ashamed of his background? We know that you cannot be held liable for your origin or punished for it and so forth, but that is something else altogether. But in my opinion you should not be ashamed—why should you? If I were Jewish I would admit it proudly. But I am not—I don't have anything to explain.

At almost all the press conferences I would be handed a few scraps of paper with anonymous questions that had an anti-Semitic flavor. Here is a mild example: "Millions of Poles are waiting for this answer. When will you finally expel all the European-jews (Jews written without the capital) from the Citizens' Parliamentary Caucus and the government?"

All visible examples of racism and intolerance must be exposed and publicly branded for what they are. That is why I often read such questions, even though they were anonymous.

Wałęsa's critics have this to say on the subject:

Adam Michnik: I say this on the basis of my long, personal acquaintance with Lech Wałęsa: He was never an anti-Semite or a populist. He considered both ideas idiotic. By mouthing nonsense about the "eggheads" and separating people into Jews and non-Jews he did make a bow toward those nursing anti-intellectual populism and anti-Semitic phobias. Now those people will support Wałęsa's run for the presidency.

Wałęsa says: "I am a pure Pole, born here." Then there must be some "impure" Poles born elsewhere. Wałęsa is critical of the Western press saying "some hands have a long reach." Where have I heard this language of obsession and insinuation?

The leader of the Democratic Right Forum holds a similar opinion.

Aleksander Hall: I am convinced that just a year ago, at any rally, Wałęsa would have cut short and jeered any kind of anti-Semitic phobias. Today he does not give unequivocal answers. He is using the subject in the election game. He is winking at the public. He says: "I am a Pole going back generations, but I am not an anti-Semite." I have no doubt that he is not anti-Semitic, but I do think that he is using the subject for political purposes.

I share both of these viewpoints.

3

I was misunderstood! ... The devil has twisted it all around.
—Lech Wałęsa, speaking on Polish Radio, August 24, 1990

Wałęsa's typical day at the Solidarity headquarters would go something like this:

He is picked up at his home each morning at 9:30 and arrives at work precisely at 9:45. He enters the office bursting with energy, exchanging casual greetings. He throws his briefcase on the big oak desk and hangs his sheepskin coat in the closet. Then he sits in the swivel chair. The keys jingle as he opens the center desk drawer to its limit, neatly pressing his tie into his rounded middle.

The day now begins in earnest. The mood of the chief will no doubt influence all who will cross the threshold of the office. There is much running about. The telephones begin to ring. Doors slam. The espresso machine is brewing coffee; water is boiling for the chief's customary mint tea.

Pusz, secretary to the chief, does not have to leave his office to know that Lech has arrived; he knows it telepathically. In a second he enters Lech's office and begins to relate current matters: There were calls ... they tried to get one over on us ... there's an important person coming ... it will be necessary to visit Warsaw. Then it's Wałęsa's turn: sign this, take that ... deliver ... Mazowiecki ... the Citizens' Committee ... they will bring it ... the plane tickets ... Kaczyński ... the Left ... clever rascals ... It is a crucial moment. It will decide if the level of tension in the office will rise above the normal daily high.

The newspapers have already been placed upon Wałęsa's desk. Articles about him and other important items have been marked by the press bureau with a bright colored pen. If the *Gazeta Wyborcza* has been kind to Lech the tension may decrease somewhat. There will be no need to issue statements or corrections.

The mint tea is brought in. Should one of the secretaries hear a compliment on the order of "You certainly don't look your age today" or "Looks like you've finally lost some weight," it can be presumed that the day at 24 Wały Piastowskie in Gdańsk will be relatively calm. But one can never be sure.

After 10:00 the journalists, businesspeople, ambassadors, and delegations start to arrive. Photographs are taken, camera shutters clicking as handshakes are exchanged. Coffee is served in Kashubian mugs bearing the Solidarity logo. Wałęsa is persuasive. He stresses the opportunities, the need for rapid investment ... hurry, hurry, there's money in the streets, and if you don't grab it others will get it first. He talks about Poland's place in Europe, reforms, pluralism, the struggle with monopolies ... The visitors listen, nod their heads, make a stab at humor. They understand it all, they share and admire his views, and of course they will try to do everything in their power to ...

Some of the businessmen in starched white collars have brought along their wives who are feigning interest in the conversation. Meanwhile, they are taking the opportunity to look around the office of the famous person whom they know only from NBC newsclips and the cover of *Newsweek*.

There is a mahogany bookshelf groaning under the weight of mementos and gifts—medals, commemorative albums, banners, plaques, cups, and statuettes—it's all in one great pile. Over the desk is the quintessential symbol of God and country: a crowned white eagle with the Virgin Mary emblazoned on its chest, trimmed with a red and white ribbon of the Polish national colors (and rather reminiscent of a road warning sign). There is a TV set in one corner. Three armchairs, a couch, and a low coffee table complete the furniture. Wałęsa likes to sit with his back to the window, a setup that drives the photographers crazy. On his right is a statuette of Piłsudski, Poland's prewar leader, placed so that it is included in every photograph.

After the official visitors leave, the regular crowd of associates arrives for a political debate. Then Wałęsa makes himself comfortable in his armchair. He stretches out his legs, drinks his now lukewarm mint tea, and speculates, discusses, decides. To act or not to act? To clear it up or leave it unresolved? To force or to persuade?

It's 2 p.m. Wałęsa is tired. His car, an Italian Lancia, is waiting outside the building. He takes his briefcase, his sheepskin, and his bodyguards. The action is as in the morning, but in reverse and at a reduced speed.

It was really impossible to tell in what mood he would come to the office. After his triumphant tour of the United States, where he was received like visiting royalty and where the highest officials nearly knelt before him, it seemed that he would return with an unshakable faith in his own infallible genius to start a round of egotistic buffoonery. Instead he came to the office in an unassuming manner, greeted everyone, and it was business as usual.

But he could be verbally abusive to those around him. He was capable of telling his own secretary to "get lost" or insulting someone in the

Lech Wałęsa meets with Ronald Reagan during his trip to the United States (photograph by Tomasz Wierzejski, *Gazeta Wyborcza*).

presence of others. Wałęsa represents the kind of leader who demands absolute obedience and complete belief in his line of thought. In time he antagonizes strong personalities and reduces the weak to the role of lackeys. He prefers to be surrounded by people over whom he can easily hold sway. He respects his opponents if they play fair. And while he holds slimy flatterers in contempt, he cherishes them, too. Cheap compliments give him pleasure, and he sees lackeys as useful creatures. They can inform, whisper, fetch, carry, do dirt—as needed—and will assume all the responsibility. They confess their guilt, then beg the master for forgiveness and leave him assured. Or they will raise the right warning flags. When necessary they will either agree or deny.

Wałęsa plays with people. He elevates some to push others down. He can crush people, drag them through the mud just to pull them out and reward them with a harness of dependence and responsibility. He does not pay attention to anyone outside his immediate group. The workers in the economic, foreign, administrative, and press offices are all devoted people. But he notices them only when there is a problem and something must be cleared up. Sometimes he will burst into a room like a meteor, just to see if everyone is working. Several times he went to the trouble of appearing at work at 8 a.m. to catch the latecomers. He took the list from the office manager and checked the names off himself. He made a scene and issued written warnings. For people who never counted their time and effort while working for him, unselfishly putting in extra hours, this was especially unpleasant, discouraging, and even humiliating. The idealistic and selfless nature of work done for Solidarity was transformed into just another office job and for very poor pay at that. This became a source of constant frustration.

One cannot expect Wałęsa to acknowledge work well done, but he will, on occasion, find words of praise. In contrast, he points out errors scrupulously and without any consideration.

Krzysztof Wyszkowski, the cofounder of free trade unions and longtime associate of Wałęsa and Mazowiecki: Wałęsa is a political machine. He is politically efficient. Therefore it is an extravagance and folly to hold against him the fact that he lacks social graces, has bad table manners, and few manners in general. He can be infuriatingly rude. Very well. But he lives the political life on all levels. When he is in the social arena he is operating politically. The important and the unimportant, all must be either won over or subdued. In this sense he has no private life.

Lech is a magnet for the mass media from around the world, from small union bulletins to huge publications with international fame, from local radio stations to global television networks. Adjacent entries in the appointment book list Pakistan, the United States, Iceland, Mexico, Japan, Brazil, Korea, New Zealand, the USSR, and Palestine ...

All types of journalists arrive. There are the humble, the self-assured, the arrogant; dilettantes, amateurs, professionals ... All are trying to be cultured and polite. They know, after all, that until the interview is recorded on tape or in a notebook, anything can happen. The real test of a journalist takes place after the interview. There are some who do not even say good-bye. That is why at the moment the interviewer crosses the threshold of the press bureau the game begins. He must get his interview because he has not traveled 3,000 miles to come back empty-handed. His publication is among the most important, most influential, most widely read, most this, most that in his part of the world. He cannot imagine not being granted an interview with Wałęsa. He has his orders and will get the interview no matter what. If the press bureau will not arrange the interview he will find a way to get it anyhow. He has been a journalist for twenty years and will not break his career on Wałęsa's press bureau.

Obnoxious journalists usually don't get interviews; the exceptions are the truly large news services where refusal would mean a public scandal. The interviews are booked several weeks in advance. Journalists who want to conduct an interview with Wałęsa should know a few simple rules, without which they could wind up getting a load of useless information.

To journalists of goodwill, then, I offer my ten commandments. After all, conducting an interview with Wałęsa is an art. It is not because he has nothing to say, just the opposite; he simply may not be in a talkative mood.

1. You must confront him immediately after entering his presence. The chief is a dynamic personality. He loves a fight; in other situations he is lost, gets bored, and clams up. In those instances he will answer questions with a word or a sentence.

2. Save yourself the trouble of expressing greetings and gratitude for being given the time for an interview. And don't bother to tell him who you are, where you are from, and who you work for. Wałęsa is not interested. Throw a sharp challenging question immediately. The chief likes to be challenged.

3. The questions must be short and to the point. They cannot suggest an answer. They must refer to current or future events. Questions that ask for a prognosis are preferable. Avoid questions that are overly complicated, introspective, or philosophical. By God, don't ask about the past. Wałęsa has a short memory.

(A certain French bigwig, sprawled on an armchair, once asked the chief: "Mr. Wałęsa, the twenty-year period 1970 to 1990—your evaluation and reflections." This was a live television interview involving a lot of high tech. The answer: "Sir! Ask me a real question, tell me what you want, and in the future be better prepared!")

4. You must be prepared both technically and mentally. I saw several interviews that were to last fifteen minutes but only lasted two because the journalist could not operate his camera properly, had problems setting the light or sound level, or started off with absurd questions.

5. Do not submit your questions in advance. Wałęsa knows that improvisation is his strong point. He would rather not know because then his answers are better.

6. Don't ask about his private life. But if you must, then do it at the end and limit yourself to no more than two questions of the "How is your wife managing with all this?" type.

7. The time for the interview is limited. At the beginning of the interview, Wałęsa usually says: "You have ten minutes." Do not get unnerved. Your skill will govern the duration of the interview. The general rule is as follows: If you ask proper questions you will receive proper answers and the interview will conclude on time. But if you start to express your own opinions, argue and debate, then you have the

chance for an interesting, long interview. There is one condition, however: You must allow yourself to be convinced, at least somewhat.

(Attractive woman journalists get an extra ten minutes. Before the chief's departure for the United States he gave an interview to a journalist from the *Washington Post*. The woman was pretty and started off by saying that on the previous day she spoke with Andrzej Gwiazda [Wałęsa's one-time rival and fierce antagonist], who said several things from which she concluded that Mr. Wałęsa was not right. This happened just before departure. On that day Wałęsa had three interviews and a number of other matters on his schedule. The conversation, a sharp debate, lasted not twenty minutes but an hour. Afterward an exhausted Wałęsa invited the lady back for an afternoon rematch. In all, the interview lasted an hour and a half. It was a record. She turned out to be an excellent psychologist. If you aren't a beautiful woman, a feat difficult for men to pull off, then bring one along.)

8. Be sure of yourself; do not show stress or nervousness.

9. Dress as befits the occasion.

10. Present a copy of your publication to the chief only at the end of the interview. If you do it at the start then his attention will be focused on the publication and not on his answers. Do not take photographs at the moment of presentation. If you do it will be treated as an attempt to obtain "piratical advertising."

Wałęsa gets many critical comments from a wide range of people of various backgrounds and sensibilities. He is the only Polish leader to interact with such a cross-section of society even though he never attended a diplomatic school but is only a trade school graduate. In the popular imagination he functions as a person who has no barriers between himself and society. Therefore, at least formally, everyone is his partner. Almost every Pole would probably like to be Wałęsa. But on the other side of the coin, just as anyone can imagine himself to be Wałęsa, then anyone can criticize and castigate him without the least embarrassment ("after all, he's just a common peasant and an unmannered yokel"). This is why national criticism of Wałęsa is often aggressive and far too severe when set against his transgressions.

The chief has created his own style. Solidarity was a grassroots movement that required a worker's style. If the intelligentsia had doubts as to Wałęsa's person, these doubts were dispersed by the conviction that this was what the masses wanted. Wałęsa is used to a light touch; he does not take criticism well, even when it is offered in a kindly and constructive manner. He pays no attention to his own behavior, even when he knows that all eyes are upon him. But he does pay attention to the comments in the daily press—up to a point. He greedily devours every mention of his name yet never draws lessons from the criticisms.

Lech Wałęsa speaks to a large crowd at a Solidarity rally (photograph by Sławomir Sierzputowski, *Gazeta Wyborcza*).

From the middle of 1990, critical commentary began appearing in the press, notably in the Western press. This was unusual, as up to that time the Western press had been favorable toward Wałęsa.

But the power of habit in Wałęsa is stronger than the desire for better press. Even U.S. presidents (perhaps because they are presidents) do not allow themselves the luxury of ignoring the media the way Wałęsa does.

President George Bush met with the press on nearly a daily basis and tried to be constantly available. The Bush-Gorbachev summit at Malta was so arranged that news from it could make the morning edition of most U.S. daily newspapers. When Wałęsa gives an interview, he grants an audience. He cannot keep distance between himself and authors of critical articles. He simply would get insulted. On a list of antagonists (handwritten on a scrap of paper), he included — (after Mazowiecki, Geremek, Michnik, and Jaruzelski) the following journalists: Aleksander Małachowski (for a very critical essay in *Po Prostu* [Simply][1] in which he proposed Mazowiecki as a candidate for president), Passent (for the same sin committed on the pages of *Polityka*), and Jerzy Waldorff, a well known music critic (for an unknown offense).

At press conferences he treats journalists almost scornfully, saying "You are to write what Lech Wałęsa has to say to the people and write about what troubles the people—so that the government, Prime Minister Mazowiecki, would know. This is why I asked you here." But at the same time he seems to fear journalists. Going to each meeting he would ask if the press would be there. But he could still say, "Reporters, you are not writing it right."

The press conference given on August 30, 1990, was typical. At the onset Andrzej Drzycimski, my successor, reminded the press that the terms anti-Semite, populist, destabilizing factor, and demagogue, should not be used in conjunction with Wałęsa's name. Then Wałęsa took the podium.

> I would like to tell you all the following. I do not wish that, as of today, anyone should write that Wałęsa is a populist, that Wałęsa is an anti-Semite, that Wałęsa wants to split the current government and is against Prime Minister Mazowiecki. If you do so then I will make you prove all the things that you write and publish, I will make you show these problems. If you cannot prove these things at the press conference, at the meetings, then you may not write about them, because they are not so. Much is said to spite me, but no truth is said at all. I would like to see proof for the things you write, or don't write them. I am ready to show everyone that these things are all untrue and are out of place. I demonstrated it in Rome, and I will prove it in all the other places I visit. Soon I will be in the United States and in other places, and in time I will show that those who wrote those things lied. There! The challenge is given. ... How did you like the lecture! Did I insult anyone? I am trying to insult you on purpose, to get you to start a discussion. This is the only way we can talk things out!

Arkadiusz Rybicki: Lech thinks in a manner that is both too deep and too complicated for his tongue to express. The lack of education holds him back. That is why he expresses himself in a simple way. His career is founded on the fact that he was able to say the very basic things. He stood on the [shipyard] gate and called things by their real names, thus earning the admiration of the intellectuals. The intellectuals—perhaps I am oversimplifying—had a moral hangover because during the administration of Edward Gierek[2] and later they tried to paper over the brutality and emptiness of communism. Warsaw specialized in the creation of newspeak. Today, real freedom has permitted people to call things by their real names using the good Polish language. Wałęsa, in this regard, has not changed, and all his associates know it well. Now, debate with him is often an invitation to fight. One could clarify the phrase *president with an ax* or take it seriously and treat it as a sign of extremism. Wałęsa has a grudge against his friends who should know what he meant but who are playing dumb.

Lech Wałęsa at one of his many press conferences (photograph by Tomasz Wierzejski, *Gazeta Wyborcza*).

At one point in May 1990 he was so affected by the press that he ordered me to issue a statement in which I was to criticize reporters for the tendentious manner in which they presented his words. Wałęsa himself wrote the draft. To any press spokesman such a statement would mean disaster, as anyone who fights the entire press corps loses. I refused to sign the statement. Later, the text was edited by a journalist from the *Tygodnik Gdański* (Gdańsk weekly). Pusz signed the statement saying that he would rather do it than let Wałęsa dig himself into a hole. Fortunately, after much discussion and pleading Lech decided not to release the text, which said in part

> Lech Wałęsa is known as a speaker who during the broad clarification and explanation of his ideas uses picturesque stylistic phrases. He does it partly to give some color to his speech and partly to satisfy journalists so that they may use his quotes and comment more readily. Unfortunately, some journalists have gone too far in interpreting or even misstating his comments. This has caused some unfavorable public reaction. When Lech Wałęsa speaks about "political war" among the power elite and has in mind the necessity of admitting new people with fresh ideas and approaches into the government, his antagonists have the tendency to scream that "Wałęsa has declared war on the government." When he uses the word axe when speaking about the necessity of putting strict curbs on

all types of excesses and chicanery, there is a cry that he wants to launch a coup against democracy the way Piłsudski did in 1926.

Wałęsa Is For, and Even Against

The foregoing sentence typifies his ability to circumvent all uncomfortable political choices. "I am for, and even against" is the synthesis of Wałęsa's political game. It is not just for unclear situations but for everyday use. Often this culminates in such statements as, "I am the biggest opponent of nuclear generating plants, but ..." appended by some arguments in favor of nuclear energy. Or "I am the strongest supporter of democracy in the world, but ..." and here follows a lecture that justifies undemocratic practices, the abuse of authority, and so on.

When in September 1990 I asked Wałęsa if he still supported the government, asking for a negative or an affirmative reply, he said that in theory he supported it but in practice he did not. When I asked for an explanation of that statement he said, "You have to understand me in two ways."

Wałęsa is not afraid to express unpopular ideas, but only if, in his judgment, there is good reason for it. In effect it is difficult to say what his views are. It seems that he never really gave it much thought, sensing perhaps that his absorption into one of the political camps would cause a decline in his popularity. He knows that the Right will always see him as a firm anti-Communist because he, and no one else, turned the Eastern bloc upside down. For the centrists he will always be the stabilizing influence that halts radical moves, a man who favors only peaceful means of dissent. For the Left he will always be the ideal embodiment of the fighter for so-called social justice. He is of the people and stands at the head of a great labor movement. Wałęsa has such capacity that all see in him the man they want to see. Is this Wałęsa's great secret? It certainly is an important factor, because the truth about him is extremely complicated and cannot be generalized.

Lech does not look deeply into the meaning of the words and phrases he uses. At a December 1989 meeting with the leader of the French socialists, Pierre Mauroy, he started an amateurish discussion on the various meanings of the word socialism. The Frenchman, a political animal whose main purpose for coming to Gdańsk was to get favorable publicity, was very sensitive to words, especially that one. The swarm of French journalists was waiting for something sensational to happen. Wałęsa, as usual, had a lot to say and did not care to hear much of anything. His visitor said few things, but he hit the mark. In an unfortunate turn of phrase, Wałęsa admitted to socialist tendencies, which in Poland were considered an ideological link to the failed

Communist regime. It sounded hollow. He lost face and credibility; Mauroy walked away triumphant.

Wałęsa is not fond of attending meetings with international diplomats. He sees little difference among the diplomats who hold rank below that of head of state and treats them all alike—he talks at them incessantly. He has the impression that what he says is more important than what he hears. In the context of sporadic meetings with diplomats of the lower ranks, such behavior undoubtedly makes Wałęsa appear to be a dynamic and decisive person and the facts he reveals to be controversial but interesting and attractive.

But during important meetings the use of this form of address (that is, a monologue) is detrimental to Wałęsa, keeping him from gaining any knowledge about his opposite or what he has to say. A textbook example of this behavior was his meeting with the Japanese ambassador, which took place before the Japanese prime minister visited Poland. The ambassador wanted to present the topics his prime minister wished to discuss with Wałęsa. But Wałęsa interrupted him after he had announced his intentions. The meeting lasted an hour. Wałęsa droned on, not allowing the ambassador to open his mouth. In the end, Wałęsa got tired, learned nothing, and altogether missed the point of the meeting, informing the ambassador of what he wanted to discuss at the later meeting. It was as if he had mistaken the ambassador for the prime minister and told him everything he had to say.

Wałęsa usually gets his information on the run because, as is well known, he does not like to devote time to reading books. He said that he learned about the foolhardiness of taking written words to heart when his attempt to embellish a speech by quoting directly from a book backfired: Instead of inspiring his audience, he filled with fear all those who take Poland's interests to heart. The definition—"Democracy is the permanent war of everyone against everyone else"—caused a huge furor. Lech's conclusion: "I'll never read another book."

Bądkowski wrote in 1981, "I see him as a man of instinct, not of intellect. To be sure, in my opinion, he is a man of considerable intelligence, but he has never devoted himself to improving and developing it." Wałęsa, then, is forced to make up for this by learning as he goes. He remembers what others say, and if he likes the remarks, he will probably repeat them without being aware of their source. In time he begins to believe that he invented them. He uses certain favorite and effective phrases so often that those around him never doubt their authorship.

He loves to use numbers (usually astronomically large ones) without restraint. A French diplomat who visited Gdańsk was treated to a theory that France would soon be overrun by 10 million Chinese, Vietnamese, and Koreans who would arrive there with the intention of settling. The whole of Europe will be deluged by a wave of 100 million refugees if the Western nations will not support the economies of nations that have freed themselves from communism. The great democratic revolution will reach the countries of the Far East and its inhabitants who, seeking a better standard of living, will invade Europe with banners proclaiming freedom and equality.

Then there were the 10,000 Western companies that Wałęsa was going to "pair off" with their Polish counterparts before 1989. And the 500 political parties that were to spring up during the first phase of democracy in Poland. And finally there was the 99 (later 90, and still later 80) percent of the vote that Lech Wałęsa, presidential candidate, would receive from the people of Poland—and the maximum of 35 percent that Mazowiecki would get. But his weakness in arithmetic is a relatively innocent quality in comparison to his slips of the tongue, malapropisms, and linguistic accidents.

Lech has a large supply of choice sayings and folk wisdom, enough to fill a book. One such saying describes small family firms as "father, capitalist; mother, labor union; son, proletarian." Another refers to con artists: "They would like to drink blood but don't want to puncture the skin." Some others: "Today the elites are playing ping-pong and the public is trying to keep an eye on the ball"; "Who is better, a chess master or a boxing champion?"; "At the margins of democracy there always must be some manipulation"; "The best discoveries are made by amateurs; I am an amateur." I could go on forever.

When I took over the office of press spokesman from Nowina-Konopka, he wanted to make me aware of the great responsibility that went with the position. He told me how he had to squirm and twist after Lech said that it was a scandal how little French investment was committed to Poland. The French were upset, and they managed to corner Konopka at home. Several officials were suddenly on the phone asking for an immediate explanation. The conversation was to be broadcast live. The French had their own interpreter. Finally, the goodwill of the French, roundabout explanations, arguments about the chief's way of talking, and appeals to French-Polish friendship (Napoleon, Józef Poniatowski, and Marie Skłodowska-Curie)[3] took care of the problem.

The Poles living in Lithuania will not forget or forgive Lech's statement on Soviet TV, when he said that their expatriate community should be satisfied with using the Polish language "in their kitchens and churches." Czesław Okińczyc, a Polish activist in Lithuania, told me that this clip was shown many times by the TV network. One ill-advised statement badly damaged the trust of the Lithuanian Poles toward

Wałęsa and Solidarity, supporting the false impressions that they had been abandoned by their home country.

Knowing that Lech may not always say what he means to express and aware of the journalists' tendency to take advantage of this weakness, Mirek Kowalewski, my colleague in the press bureau, and I always taped all his comments to the press. Thanks to this we were able to deny a statement Wałęsa supposedly uttered that appeared in the Swedish afternoon paper *Expressen*. Lesse Persson, a journalist on friendly terms with Lech, probably through an error in translation wrote that Wałęsa said that Poland needed a dictatorship.

We also had on tape a statement to the Dutch weekly *Elsevier* from March 28, 1990. After Lech's prophetic conclusion that the only solution to the problems of the Soviet Union would be dissolution and then a reunion on a voluntary basis, he made a now famous statement about Germany: "I am again convinced that Germany has drawn conclusions [from World War II] and Europe has drawn conclusions as well. And I can say an unpopular thing. If once again Germany should risk destabilizing Europe, then there would be no division of Germany—it would simply be blown off the map of Europe. With the kind of technology that exists, with the kind of experiences we have had, there can be no other way— and the Germans know it."

A month later, this statement made its way into the West German press. Michał Jaranowski, the German correspondent for *Życie Warszawy*, wrote on June 26, 1990:

> The statement shocked the political order on the Rhine. First to protest was Heinrich Lummer, a CDU [Christian Democratic Union] representative to the Bundestag. He sent an open letter asking for an explanation. Some of the newspapers printed the letters from incensed readers. Silesian Youth, an exiles organization, put forth a request to the Nobel Peace Prize committee to rescind the prize once given to the chief of Solidarity. From the government offices in Bonn one could catch the drift that the *Elsevier* article was noticed and noted. To put it bluntly—Polish interests in Germany were hurt, while Lech Wałęsa lost a great deal of his popularity.

A large number of letters came into the press bureau. All asked, or demanded, an explanation. The letters varied from the borderline anti-Polish to pro-Polish, the latter suggesting that the matter was a misunderstanding. Lech did not want to use the explanation prepared by the press bureau. He expounded on the motives of the insistent Dutch journalist and his own fatigue; he also suggested that the magazine purposely twisted his words. His defense was not very convincing, even coming from the man who is a proponent of Polish-German understanding. Speaking as the most prominent politician in Poland, Wałęsa had on occasion stated that the separation of the two Germanies was an unnatural condition. In a conversation with Hans-Dietrich Genscher and Horst Teltschik,[4] he predicted the demolition of the Berlin Wall. And now he had to explain his anti-German tendencies.

4

You are mistaken.
—Lech Wałęsa, to his press spokesman, June 11, 1991

Three weeks after the Solidarity congress came a moment in which I had to make a personal declaration. I could no longer pretend that I was indifferent while in my opinion Lech was making one blunder after another.

I thought about the form my statement should take. I decided it would best be put in writing. This would allow me to give a full and precise explanation of all my arguments. I was afraid that Wałęsa would misinterpret my intentions and treat the memorandum as a personal attack, the mean-spirited comments of a punk who had gone crazy. Not wanting to risk the action by myself, I decided to bring Pusz into the meeting with Wałęsa, counting on the impression that the opinions of two close associates would make on Lech.

The beginning of May 1990 was a nightmare for Lech and all the workers in the support bureaus. Nothing was happening on the domestic political scene, but everyone could feel the political tensions. (At the end of the preceding week, *Gazeta Wyborcza* had printed the results of its presidential survey, in which Wałęsa came out in fourth place.)

Lech behaved like a monster. He got mad at Pusz for arranging meetings to which Wałęsa had agreed in the first place. Ten times he allowed himself to be persuaded to make the trip to West Germany and Scandinavia for the national congress of German trade unions; ten times over he cancelled the trip. He refused to give interviews that had been scheduled weeks in advance. But eventually, after heated combat, he would relent. The culmination of this nonsense came on May 8. Lech refused to grant an interview to a Finnish paper, an interview that was to tie into his Scandinavian trip. He started yelling at me. I could not take it. I paid him back in like coin, then I turned around and left, slamming the door. I knew I did the wrong thing in allowing emotions to take control. But I also knew I had to make myself understood.

The Finnish journalists were waiting in innocent ignorance to meet the chief in my office. I was on the phone in the reception area when in came Lech with a stern expression on his face. He walked in with such energy that I had no time to react. He gave the interview, which lasted forty-five minutes instead of fifteen. He came out in a champagne mood.

It turned out that Joanna Strzemieczna, his secretary, convinced him that he should give the interview after all. Supposedly he said, "What? Kurski wants to quit? If he wants to he can; after all, he's been getting too bossy around here." I was afraid that this story would repeat itself the following morning. When I informed him about the arrival of the *New York Times* correspondent, he answered by pretending to be mad: "You were not to arrange any interviews." I explained that the interview had been slated well in advance; he told me to bring them in. The situation was defused.

I planned to have my talk with Pusz. He liked the idea of a memo to Wałęsa but later, when the chief forbade him to maintain further contact with Michnik, concluded that it was crazy and that there was no point in our going to see the chief together. He said that there was no chance of appealing to him. My diagnosis was more optimistic. I thought that there was a 5 percent chance that such an act would be crowned with success. I wrote the document over the course of several evenings. I wanted to deliver it as material for discussion, hoping that after reading it, Lech would have a private meeting with me. My hopes were in vain.

On May 13 there was to be a meeting of the Citizens' Committee in Warsaw. Lech spent the entire difficult week preceding it in seclusion; preparing for his appearance. His statements during a press conference at the Puck Mechanical Enterprise on May 10 made it easy to guess what Lech would say at the subsequent meeting. May 11, then, was the last day on which I could present my memorandum.

There was still another obstacle. Wałęsa, several times per day, will say that he believes no one, not even himself. "Don't believe Lech," he says at the rallies. He is extremely distrustful, even toward his closest associates. The effect is that Lech has scores of followers but no real friends.

In the beginning of July 1990 I had traveled to Kielce as his representative at the unveiling ceremony for the memorial tablet honoring Jews killed in a pogrom. For this long trip (which because of the mileage is profitable to the driver), I had asked for the most dependable and honest driver, an old Home Army member named Casimir, who was once a resident of the Kielce district. I preferred Casimir over Złotówa, Lech's driver, who often played the roles of doorman, valet, waiter, messenger, but chiefly informer.

The first thing that Lech asked after my return—part jokingly, part seriously, but rather grudgingly—was, "Why did you take Casimir and not Złotówa?"

"Krzysztof said that I could pick my own driver."

"You took Casimir because you knew Złotówa would tell me every-thing."

"Lech, I had no idea you spied on your own people."

He smiled in return. It was, of course, a joke, but with a double meaning. Oh, that Lech.

Three months earlier I had entered Lech's office with my manuscript. I told him that I had a matter that required a moment of quiet concentra-tion. He was preparing for his speech before the Citizens' Committee and asked if my business was important. I answered that it was, and to such a degree that should he share my viewpoint he may have to change the text of his speech.

"So important?" He became interested. He rose from behind the desk and indicated that I should take a seat. We both made ourselves comfort-able.

"You know, Lech, that I am very much like my mother,[1] who when she disagreed with you always said it to your face. The only difference is that in 1981 she was among your opponents, while I by function and convic-tion wished you the very best. I think that you are in a very difficult situation where further moves must be thought out very carefully. Krzysztof shares my belief. I wrote it all down. This is the original. I'm keeping two copies."

"Why the copies?" he asked.

"I never like to part with things I have written," I answered.

The chief accepted my gift with kindness. He said a few warm words—that he does not pick people at random, that he is banking on youth, and so on. He was calm, understanding, almost fatherly. He put the manuscript in his briefcase. We parted in friendship.

As Saturday passed I was filled with curiosity and anticipation. I imagined when Lech, during a quiet moment at home, his feet in slippers, would go to his briefcase and open the brass catches. He would probably be thinking, "What did my press spokesman write for me?" Then he would settle down on the living room sofa, turn on a lamp, and read the first words of the memo.

Lech! I have written this for you, not against you! J.K

Loyalty to one's chief includes primarily the duty to speak the truth regardless whether it is sweet or bitter, with the provision that it must be told to him first. When this is difficult to do, merely keeping silent will cause more damage than an enemy's actions. ...

Persons such as Mazowiecki and Geremek, who recently played the role of advisors, gained their own political subjectivity with the formation of the new government. To maintain and expand it they had to act reso-lutely when opposing those who had given them power, more resolutely, in fact, than they would behave in opposition to total strangers. The chief continues to treat them as advisors, yet they do not wish to be whipping boys. The triumphal visit to the United States is the moment that marked the beginning of the steady decline in Lech's popularity. ...

Why is Lech becoming less popular?

In general there are three factors at work:

1. Political—an especially unfavorable alignment
2. Sociological—new expectations by society from Lech's persona
3. Psychological—Lech's inability to locate himself in the new situation

In my opinion, the responsibility for downgrading Lech's influence should be assigned in the reverse order of that given above. That is to say that he bears the greatest responsibility. I will discuss all the factors in the order that I have listed them.

The Political Alignment

Wałęsa is outside the alignment of parliament, the government, and the president. But meanwhile he is perceived by society as the author of the change, morally obligated to support the government of Tadeusz Mazowiecki, on whose policies he has very little influence. In supporting it he automatically assumes part of the responsibility for all of its misadventures, which under the current political and economic circumstances are quite easy to come by.

Wałęsa's popularity is penalized every time the government makes an unpopular decision. A poster from the Second National Solidarity Congress portrayed Solidarity as an open umbrella over Poland. Lech Wałęsa is the umbrella stretched over the government.

The reason for the deepening shadow over the chief is that political life takes place in Warsaw, while he works out of Gdańsk. Every trip that Lech makes to the capital (he hates to leave home) is an expedition. Recently an expression of this status quo was the following item on a TV news program: "This marks the second day of a visit by Douglas Hurd in Poland. Today the political part of the trip ends. Tomorrow the British foreign minister will travel to Gdańsk."

Lech does not have a steady group of advisors. ... He is an individual locked into a single concept or his own initiative. But the things that he can initiate may not always live up to the high expectations that are associated with his person.

Lech is suffering through a political identity crisis. To date his two formulas of "an institution unto himself" and "union leader" complemented each other superbly. It is Lech's moral imperative to support the government, but his union base criticizes this. They desire the syndication of the labor union and a revindication of the chief's position.

The Expectations of Society

The social need for a national hero, one who symbolizes truth in today's world, has undergone a change. That hero is no longer Lech Wałęsa—spry, dynamic, doing political somersaults. ...

All the characteristics that were acceptable for a labor leader (and were even counted as virtues) today are a burden to the potential president.

Society, after years of totalitarian governments, has acquired an inbred distaste for authoritarian one-man rule, even though it might be the most appropriate thing and done in the name of the most noble goals, even though it might be done by Lech Wałęsa himself. ...

Lech's Psychology

The chief acts in a way that is both nervous and impulsive. His decisions are not always carefully thought out, his actions not consistent with a straight, logical political line. The chief hides his confusion in public overactivity, speaking out on just about every subject and not always with the best effect. The frequent press conferences and meetings have led to the devaluation of his words. By not letting political debaters take the podium, by talking around them, by treating them to his own political and economic theories Lech has produced a situation in which he is more eager to hear himself talk than to listen to others.

The myth of the chief's political genius and infallibility which was created by society and surroundings but has its origins in facts, has led to a situation in which he, believing in his own genius, is unable to accept that he has indeed committed errors and in a short time has lost a great deal of popularity. Popularity and politics are not governed by mathematical laws. The negative factors have been at work with doubled force in a remarkably short time. That is why attempts to make Lech aware of this type of reality are for most part doomed to failure. ...

The chief needs some friendly and well-meaning criticism just as he needs fresh air. The forest of raised arms [signifying approval] and the consecutive election to leadership of the labor union are the results of political resources gathered in the last few years. These resources are running out.

Lech is active in his personal and political lives. He is dynamic. That is why he could not reconcile himself with the proposed idea of "going to Sulejówek"[2] [taking a vacation] to wait out the unfavorable period.

(Of course I did not suggest a full withdrawal from politics. It is only necessary to decrease the intensity of one's political activity and limit oneself to the statutory functions. This would mean fewer speeches, made only to address important issues. If Wałęsa had done this after returning from the States, he would have preserved his enormous authority. He would not have had to struggle for the presidency, and, I am convinced, he would have been asked to assume the office. But

Wałęsa voluntarily resigned the role of political arbitrator. By becoming an actor on one side of the conflict, he reduced himself to a role among the many actors on the Polish political scene, where he could have been the author and director of a play called *Poland on Its Way to Democracy.* He would have accomplished his political goals just as well. The desired split in the Solidarity camp could have been accomplished in a peaceful and controlled manner. There was no need to devalue the myth, the authority, and a lifetime accomplishment. It would not have been difficult because divisions in Solidarity and the movements of the committees were already well advanced. The artificial speedup caused them to make a skewed appearance on the political scene, presenting a caricature of the divisions of left, center, right.)[3]

> By following this advice, Lech could have preserved much of his political and moral authority. But he treated all such proposals as attempts to demolish his political persona. ...
> It appears that Lech has achieved a level that may be called the rung of incompetence (which can be seen in detail during the chief's meetings with international personalities). He seems to be losing that miraculous instinct that has never before failed him and that guided him in saying the right things and acting in the correct way.
> Here (in their chronological order) are the nine cardinal sins he committed after his return from the States:
> 1. Paying homage to a philosophy of acting without communicating with the Mazowiecki government, surprising and antagonizing administration. Examples: the matter of special authority for the government, making the announcement about the early elections to the self-government organs before Mazowiecki had a chance to do so, the initiative for the withdrawal of Soviet forces from Poland. ... [See chapter 5 for more information about these examples.]

(All these proposals, though politically sound and resulting from the chief's best intentions, brought with them the beginning of a conflict with the government, because the Council of Ministers learned about them at the same time as did the public. I can only surmise that Lech was being disloyal and purposely did not inform Mazowiecki about his intentions, wanting to show the prime minister how to rule and who was more important.)

> 2. The meeting with Mieczysław Rakowski.
> 3. The silence and passivity in the matter of the guarantees for our western borders and the matter of Polish participation in the "2 + 4" [East and West Germany + United States, France, Great Britain, Soviet Union] conference.

General Wojciech Jaruzelski (photograph by Tomasz Wierzejski, *Gazeta Wyborcza*)

(Lech said little about the inviolability of Poland's Western border. When this matter was reaching its hottest stage, when his words would have had a lot of weight, he said hardly anything at all. All the subjects of the political game called for a peace treaty with the Germans; society was ready and united on the issue. Jaruzelski wore his general's uniform during a border inspection. Statements were constantly coming out of the Sejm and the senate. But Lech was silent. In politics silence can be deafening.)

4. The trivialization of Vaclav Havel's visit to Warsaw.
5. The offense given to the group of Warsaw advisors and the prime minister.
6. Absence at events that, because of their national and official significance, demanded the chief's presence. For example, his failure to attend the concert "Artists for Poland" and not making a visit to the hospital during the convalescence of Cardinal Glemp.

(Lech tried to excuse his behavior by his reluctance to appear in public with General Jaruzelski. The effect produced by his absence at the concert "Artists for Poland" was that Mazowiecki, not Wałęsa, became the hero of the evening. Meanwhile General Jaruzelski took advantage of Wałęsa's absence at the hospital and made several zealous visits to the bedside of the cardinal. Wałęsa asked me simply to send a personal get-well note. On this count he explained that he did not wish to turn the cardinal's hospital stay into an instrument of the political game.)

7. The premature confirmation of his intention to seek the presidency.
8. The lack of decisiveness and absence of a unified strategy for communication. The constant confirmation and repudiation, the offending of and apologizing to political partners (Mazowiecki and Jaruzelski, for example).
9. The anti-intellectual rhetoric.

These nine consecutive errors created an image of a phantasmagoric Lech Wałęsa who had a grudge against the entire world. ...

What Is to Be Done?

The situation demands that the chief make diametric changes in his style. Up to this time the political resources Lech collected during the last eight years worked for him. Today most of them are gone. If Lech wishes to rebuild his position, then he must work on gaining the support of the public, the way politicians everywhere in the world do. The time in which Wałęsa could get away with anything is long over.

Lech should begin to gain supporters and not offend his devoted friends. He must break out of the growing isolation. Lech has virtues that he can use in the political game. It would be well to remove the causes of conflict in the Citizens' Committee—by holding an election, for example.

Lech's anti-intellectual rhetoric is harmful; it must be discontinued. Endless talk about eggheads may lead to the conclusion that he is hung up on this topic.

Wałęsa should adopt a speaking style that is more contained and controlled. An emotional Lech looks bad, especially on a TV screen. It is important that he make fewer speeches but on significant topics and without contradicting himself.

It is bad form to show nervousness and discomfort caused by (let us hope) a momentary lack of success. He should do what he has planned, make his scheduled rounds.

Lech must rest, digest it all, look at the situation from a distance. Three days in Węsiory[4] would work wonders.

Not all is lost, but much must be recovered, and this includes the presidency. Lech can be comforted that his legend in the world has grown to such proportions that the Polish political scene is not the only stage for his public activities. He can yet do great things as a Nobel Prize winner of world renown. If he wanted to, I believe that he could easily become a leader of a world labor movement. His persona has much to offer to the Western world, which has fallen into decadence. His involvement in a world forum can open a new chapter in the history of international movements. That is why the chief should not lose his feeling of self-worth, because he has many other alternatives to going fishing.

Jarosław Kurski, press spokesman, Gdańsk, May 10, 1990.

On the morning of May 13 we rode together to the meeting of the Citizens' Committee. It was a large group, so we went in two cars. Lech was in the first, I in the second. He did not greet me, acting as if he had not seen me. I felt out of place. At a rest stop midtrip he said: "I read your letter, but I must say that you are wrong. You have a lot to learn. But it makes me happy to see that you are trying to think." We went to a restaurant for coffee. The presence of other people, Lech's son among them, made an in-depth conversation impossible. After that he never mentioned my memo.

Leopold Unger, a journalist based in Brussels and one of the few people who read my memo, said that I should measure my success by the things that did not happen. That is, if the chief did not fire me, then that was an accomplishment. Somehow he did not fire me. Instead, it seemed that he became more friendly.

It is very difficult to win a debate with Wałęsa. The moment that Lech realizes that his opponent is right, those arguments suddenly become his own. He takes on the point of view with no scruples whatsoever. Further discussion is unnecessary. That is why you can't win: Either you lose the discussion because you are wrong, or you lose because you are right.

Lech did not share any of my views. Even if he was ready to accept several of them, it did not go far enough to cause him to change his plans of the previous week and cancel the upcoming speech. I considered this speech to be Wałęsa's version of crossing the Rubicon. It was on May 13 that he spoke about the "war at the top" and the "egghead intellectuals."

The things that Lech said from the podium filled everyone with terror. Well, perhaps not everyone: Lech was supported by his new allies. Foremost was Andrzej Słowik, recently an antagonist, a representative of the National Catholic viewpoint who ran as an opposition candidate for the post of union chairman. After him was Ryszard Bender, a professor from the Catholic University of Lublin, and other representatives of the fundamental Right. Leszek Kaczyński stepped out into the corridor during the chief's speech. He did not want to upset himself.

"This is some kind of bloody horror," said Adam Michnik. "In my darkest nightmares I never expected such a monstrous turn of events! What is Lech talking about? If a year ago someone had told me that Lech would make so many enemies I would have sent that man to Tworki [a mental hospital]! Lech must have lost his instincts."

Marek Edelman, a Solidarity activist, asked rhetorically, "Can you explain to me what the chief is talking about, what this war is? Has he gone mad? Why is he doing this? I must be too stupid to understand him."

Geremek, a carefully forced smile hiding his embarrassment, admitted in the corridor that after the chief's meeting with Cyrus Vance[5] on May 19, 1990, the horrified Americans returned with the conviction that Poland was at the brink of destabilization and civil war. Lech had created this impression by using the quote that democracy was a permanent war of everyone against everyone else. Investors need stability, not frontal warfare, and Vance heard from Wałęsa a totally different message than was being broadcast by the government and the parliamentarians. Vance believed Wałęsa. He is a close friend of Zbigniew Brzeziński, who in turn is a friend of Jan Nowak-Jeziorański. Nowak-Jeziorański had been a member of the underground Home Army during World War II and acted as a secret courier, later becoming a broadcaster for Radio Free Europe. He nearly worshiped Wałęsa. He had said that Poland has two people well known around the world: Pope John Paul II and Lech Wałęsa. He said that they were a great resource that should not be squandered. After hearing a relation of events from Brzeziński, Nowak-Jeziorański, acting with the best of intentions, wrote a sharp letter to Wałęsa presenting his own views on the matter. The envelope was carefully sealed and marked "Deliver to Addressee Personally."

The correspondence was delivered by Jacek Taylor, a lawyer who considers Nowak-Jeziorański a member of his own family. Taylor told me that Nowak-Jeziorański was tremendously upset and moved and expressed this indignation in his letter. Lech read the message carefully.

Lech Wałęsa greets Zbigniew Brzeziński (photograph by Sławomir Sierzputowski, *Gazeta Wyborcza*).

He smiled, folded it in two, and placed it in his pocket. This showed that the letter contained criticism, as other letters stay in the office. I learned later that Brzeziński tried to dissuade Nowak-Jeziorański from writing so honestly. As could be seen, his attempts were to no avail.

A few months later, on the ninth anniversary of the creation of Solidarity as a recognized labor union, Nowak-Jeziorański came to Gdańsk. Lech was informed about the visit, but he showed no desire to meet with the "courier from Warsaw." Nowak-Jeziorański's fascination with Lech evaporated after he heard the opinions of prominent U.S. politicians who were also in Gdańsk. After his conversation with Lech on the topic of the "war at the top," Henry Kissinger recommended that U.S. industrialists hold up their investments for six months. He was convinced that Poland was at the brink of collapse.

I got an especially discouraging impression from the meeting between Wałęsa and President Richard von Weizsäcker of Germany. It lasted forty minutes. During the first five the president showed interest in Lech's monologue. Then he grew indifferent. He started looking around the room. In the end he openly ignored Wałęsa. Lech meanwhile was moving in closer to the president, sitting at the very edge of his seat. Weizsäcker drummed his fingers on the couch; he looked at the ceiling. Lech droned on. I was seated at the chief's desk trying to take notes. But the president was silent. The situation was so explicit that I started wondering whether Weizsäcker was overdoing it.

Lech was always hurt by the accusation that he could not handle conversations with diplomats. "Why don't Geremek and Mazowiecki defend me?" he asked. "After all, they know that I would not let them speak because they were not part of my concept. But the meetings always came out fine. ... Mazowiecki himself asked me, 'Lech, let me say something.' I agreed and Mazowiecki spoke to the pope."

Leopold Unger wrote about the way the Gdańsk meetings were received in the June 1990 issue of *Kultura* (Culture).[6]

> Some of the important foreign visitors left Gdańsk with mixed feelings, to put it delicately. According to my sources of information, such men as Cyrus Vance or James Baker, the U.S. secretary of state; the West German president, von Weizsäcker; the Belgian (and European) socialist leader [Guy] Spitaels; and other western diplomats in Warsaw who recently were still very friendly to him, did not hide the more or less bad impression they received from their last contact with Wałęsa. They were not pleased with the methods that he or his advisors were practicing in their politics.
>
> Naturally, Wałęsa can hold the opinion that Poles are more important to him than foreigners, but he knows that he cannot disregard this phenomenon.

The first serious warning was brought from Washington on June 12 by Dan Rostenkowski, a congressman of Polish descent. He insisted on meeting Wałęsa alone. Lech said that he had no secrets before the press and that everything he said was public. The dumbfounded Rostenkowski had to make his statement in veiled form, but Wałęsa still did not agree. Rostenkowski's message was simple: Investment needs political stability.

It is difficult to assess how much damage the "war at the top" and Wałęsa's other statements had caused. Certainly, foreign financial interests became more cautious when looking for investment opportunities and turned their attention to Czechoslovakia and Hungary. Fortunately in Poland, a decoupling of the economic and political arenas did take place. As a result, Poland was first among the former Eastern bloc nations to experience economic growth and now seems to be the most advanced in applying reforms.

When in 1980 Borusewicz, Gwiazda, and others said democratically that we should thank Mazowiecki and Geremek at the shipyard, accept their letter of support, and send them back to Warsaw, I said no. And this was the beginning of my reign as dictator. If I had not done this then Mr. Mazowiecki would still be writing for Więź [Link, a Catholic opposition magazine] and Geremek would not be Geremek. They had no feel for politics.
    —Lech Wałęsa, in an interview with *Gazeta Wyborcza*, May 31, 1990

In August 1980, with the formation of Solidarity, a marriage of dissimilar interests took place. The differences among the union's adherents were many—life-style, character, philosophy, temperament, methods of thinking, everything. It was a union born not of reason but of sympathy and respect. Even though the times were not the best, eight years passed in harmony and understanding. The common goal—the defeat of the Communist party and the rerouting of Polish politics onto democratic tracks—erased all differences.

Mazowiecki came to assist the Solidarity labor union as it was being born at the Gdańsk shipyard, bringing with him the support of the lay Catholic opposition. He had spent many years working within the system as far as the rules allowed. By backing the strikers, he embarked on a new phase in his career. His considerable experience started paying dividends—the techniques of negotiation and compromise were having effect. But his philosophy and agenda were different from Wałęsa's.

When success was near, a crisis occurred. On July 7, 1989, Archbishop Dąbrowski tried to reconcile the sides. It was to no avail. Exactly on the tenth anniversary of the creation of the union and the beginning of their political cooperation, Mazowiecki and Wałęsa went their separate ways in a Catholic manner. Bishop Gocłowski blessed the parting. One of them said that they should be opponents, not enemies. But the result was far different.

Krzysztof Wyszkowski remembers: The mutual fascination between Wałęsa and Mazowiecki was superficial from the very beginning. Mazowiecki is an old realist, a man who for decades has coexisted with the Communists without losing his own integrity (a hellishly difficult feat). He knew how much effort and strength of character are necessary to survive and remain an honest patriot. Mazowiecki could do it. But the extraordinary effort that goes into preserving his own integrity prevents him from moving forward. He is like a turtle: Because he has armor, he is excellent on defense, but he can't run up to attack. Wałęsa is not weighed down. The meeting in 1980 was a meeting between a Pole who for years had lived in slavery and a Pole who aspired to freedom. To an old Pole there is nothing more beautiful than to see a young Pole who is able to lead and to fight.

The situation pushed them toward each other. At the time it was not possible to win complete freedom; that is why Wałęsa had to listen to Mazowiecki's advice. This advice tempered the demands of society. Mazowiecki drew strength from this great movement whose symbol was Wałęsa. It was a fascinating turn of events, until freedom was won.

When the possibility of winning full freedom appeared, there was only room for one, for the one who desired total freedom. The other said, "It's not time yet; slowly; only I can govern in the newly won freedom because I know what it was like to be a slave."

Mazowiecki thought that one had to enter into an honest compromise with the Communists. For him, compromise was a biological necessity. For Wałęsa, compromise was only a tactical necessity, a knot that would bind him for the shortest possible time.

Then came the May 1988 strike, and it immediately acquired historical dimensions. The negotiations were taking place at a very low level—just to obtain recognition for the strike committee as a partner in the talks. Mazowiecki arrived as a negotiator representing the church. He was present when a minimal understanding with the shipyard directors was reached. He was interested in the barest commitment, a beginning, the first thread of a greater future compromise—a recognition of the strike by the government. At the same time Andrzej Celiński [an activist from the democratic opposition movement and one of Wałęsa's advisors], extended a proposal for an honorable exit with the rejection of the small compromise.

Without even considering the means of ending the strike, we had to think about the very important question of getting the striking young workers to leave. They had to be softened up somehow.

The day before they were to leave, a demonstration was organized. Mazowiecki does not know or understand workers. Among the strikers were several hundred young, bitter, hot, brave people. Mazowiecki thought that they were immune to argument. But Wałęsa knew well that although they were hard, arguments were getting through to them. He was aware that the brave also know fear. He had

Lech Wałęsa and other Solidarity activists leave the Gdańsk shipyard at the conclusion of the May 1988 strike (photograph by Anna Bohdziewicz, *Gazeta Wyborcza*).

the feeling of being in control over them. Mazowiecki could not understand this. He thought that they needed more convincing. It was unnecessary. When Celiński tried [to persuade the workers to go], they nearly ripped him apart. Wałęsa took upon himself the task of preparing the strikers to leave. He took the podium and started to talk. He created an atmosphere that was to his liking. He could see that contact had been established. He could feel that on the next day he would be able to convince the young workers. For that day the plan was [to avoid] defeatist moods. It was important to play the atmosphere to the end. He finished with a shout, "There is no freedom without Solidarity! We will not surrender!"

In the hall there was enthusiasm, cheers. Wałęsa descended from the podium. He approached Mazowiecki, and then there was a collision of two worlds, of two epochs. Mazowiecki was enraged. He started screaming, "What have you done! How could you! This makes no sense!"

I have never seen him in such a state. He used very sharp and decisive words.

And then we saw that there was a conflict between the two camps.

At that moment we felt that we had won and should march out with our victory. We saw that the Reds were knocked out. But Mazowiecki could not believe it! He was still bound to the philosophy of Znak [Sign, a Catholic opposition organization]—the philosophy of small steps and minuscule compromises.

This moment shook both of them. After eight years of excellent cooperation, suddenly there was pronounced conflict.

On the next day Wałęsa purposely continued to taunt Mazowiecki. Whenever they passed each other he would say loudly, "There is no freedom without Solidarity." On the following day things calmed down. But I think that there remained an indelible mark on the relationship between Mazowiecki and Wałęsa.

During the course of the presidential campaign, Mazowiecki would use the episode from May 1988 to illustrate Wałęsa's unpredictability, saying, "Even on the last day he still tried to fire up the mood."

Then there was the creation of the Citizens' Committee, the "Round Table," and the June elections to the Sejm and senate. Mazowiecki refused to be a candidate because of the differences that came into sharp focus over an issue raised by Aleksander Hall, a future minister in the Mazowiecki government. Hall thought that the committee should permit representatives of other opposition political groups—for example, the Dziekania[1] political club, the Kraków Industrial Association, the *Głos* (Voice)[2] community, the Christian Democratic group led by Siła-Nowicki, and people such as Wiesław Chrzanowski and Stanisław Stomma—to take part in the elections. Mazowiecki supported Hall's concept.

At that time Mazowiecki was less than delighted with the growing influence of the successor faction to the Workers' Defense Committee in which Geremek was a leading figure. At this time, Wałęsa, in contrast, was closest to this group. Wałęsa wanted Geremek to become the leader of Solidarity representatives in the Sejm and Mazowiecki to head the senate. Although Wałęsa eventually persuaded Geremek to run, he had no such luck with Mazowiecki. After countless verbal battles, Wałęsa finally said, "Tadeusz, if you will not be a candidate, then our ways must part."

Despite his desire to hold a seat in the government, Mazowiecki, who had a long history of parliamentary practice in the right leaning Znak group, refused to compromise his principles by associating himself with the leftist philosophy of the post-KOR faction. During his time as a deputy he tried to convene a commission in the Sejm that would look into the events, and their causes, in the Gdańsk area during December 1970.[3] Because of that stand he was denied a mandate for another term. His return to the Sejm would have brought personal satisfaction and a vindication of his politics.

Lech Wałęsa surprised Tadeusz Mazowiecki by selecting him for the position of
prime minister (photograph by Tomasz Wierzejski, *Gazeta Wyborcza*).

The future prime minister was convinced that the next four years
would be a period of marginal politics. He envisioned political opposition
as a laborious process. He would continue as the editor of *Tygodnik
Solidarność* (Solidarity weekly). On its pages in August 1989 he rejected
Michnik's visionary idea—"Your [the Communists'] president; our
[Solidarity's] prime minister."

In the beginning everyone assumed that Wałęsa would become prime
minister. But Wałęsa would not let either Jarosław Kaczyński or Adam
Michnik persuade him. Later he explained his position:

I would like to apologize that it took me so long to enter the government.
The reason for this was not that I lacked the intelligence and would not
have been able to manage. I would have been able to manage. But I knew
that it would have been extremely difficult. I wanted to stay with the
people. I fully expected that it might not work the first time and that we
might have to try as many as three times. I wanted to be with the masses.
Not because I was making the smart move, but I did not want the masses
to be alone, to prevent them from doing stupid things, because in difficult
situations this is easy to do. I stayed so that I could lead them through the
reforms."

In another interview he said: "I stayed with the workers."

I think that Wałęsa was already measuring himself for the presidency, which would eventually be vacated by Jaruzelski. He could not envision any other role than a primary one for himself in the new government.

Leszek Kaczyński: Jarek [Jarosław Kaczyński] was chief among Mazowiecki's backers. I, at one time, backed Kuroń.

The decision that it was going to be Mazowiecki was made in an automobile belonging to the Democratic party [SD] on the way from the Europejski Hotel to the Sejm. On that day [August 17] there was a meeting of the Citizens' Parliamentary Caucus, at which Jarek would report on the matter of the coalition of Solidarity, SD, and ZSL [United Peasant Party].[4] He was abused without mercy. Everyone was against this idea, and especially the fact that my brother was implementing it. Geremek and his people questioned the idea. The debate raged. We became convinced that Wałęsa would have to be brought in.

We knew that Lech was coming to Warsaw. A Western journalist whispered that he was already here. We grabbed the first car. Indeed he was at the Europejski Hotel. He and Mazowiecki were having supper together. We took him by the arm and got into the car. During the trip Lech said, "Well, let's make the old man the prime minister."

We drove to the Sejm, and there Lech delivered one of his best speeches, which began with the words "I did not yearn for you." He crushed his audience absolutely flat.

Krzysztof Pusz: Before the Kaczyński brothers came to the Europejski Hotel, Lech turned to Mazowiecki, "Tadeusz, you will be the prime minister." Mazowiecki was stunned. He was completely surprised. The magnitude of the surprise can be judged from the fact that he came to convince Wałęsa to abandon the concept of "Your president, our prime minister" on the grounds that it was too risky, too hurriedly formulated. Mazowiecki, at least for the sake of principle, had to express doubt in his own candidacy. After a long pause he said, "Me, Lech?"

Pusz, however, believes that in reality the proposal impressed Mazowiecki. When Lech departed for the Sejm with the Kaczyński brothers, Mazowiecki stood over the uncleared dinner dishes with his head bowed. "Krzysztof, how can I be a prime minister having Wałęsa on one side and Jaruzelski on the other? After all, your chief will be butting into everything."

At that moment Wałęsa was speaking before the Sejm. He proclaimed that on the following day the decision would be made on the subject of the prime minister. It would be one of the three people: Geremek, Kuroń, or Mazowiecki.

On the next day Wałęsa met with Jaruzelski. A while later the general received Mazowiecki. The future prime minister, after departing Belweder Palace, went directly to Wałęsa to tell him that the appointment would be announced on the following day.

Why Mazowiecki?

Krzysztof Wyszkowski: Wałęsa knew the measure of his own leadership. He knew that he directed everything, and it did not occur to him that Mazowiecki would emancipate himself. He underestimated Mazowiecki but was stuck with him.

Arkadiusz Rybicki: Wałęsa saw an alliance forming in Warsaw, one on which he would have no influence should Geremek become prime minister. Jaruzelski would be president, and the first violins would be people close to the OKP presidium. I am sure that there were whispers that Geremek would not be acceptable to the church. That is why Wałęsa chose a man whom he thought weak. Of course he made a mistake. Mazowiecki is a dyed-in-the-wool politician. He is not a puppet, even though he is slow and indecisive at times. He is a man who stands on a solid political foundation.

Leszek Kaczyński: We had an unclear idea that a coalition between Solidarity and the PZPR was forming. Michnik denies it to this day. Lityński confirmed it. Kuroń says that he did not know about it. But I think that it is a fact.

That is why Geremek was treated as the eventual head of this alliance. Moreover, we knew that Geremek was unhappy that Jarosław Kaczyński got the job of assembling the Solidarity-SD-PSL coalition. Finally, starting in July, we began to observe from Gdańsk a tendency among the leadership of the OKP not to discuss matters but to take some definite political steps. This center of power became entirely autonomous, and this was the first source of tension.

What were Mazowiecki's virtues? He had a good relationship with the church. He was practically an outsider. He was not in parliament. He had a well-known name. He was the main coordinator of the Round Table discussion. He is a serious politician. We have thought (but we were wrong) that as prime minister he would be forced to re-create the Solidarity coalition and bring in a part of its leaders (the people from Gdańsk) and some of the OKP (Warsaw) people into the government. Our first desire was that the government should unite us

Mazowiecki's face reflected the cares and woes of all Poles (photograph by Tomasz Wierzejski, *Gazeta Wyborcza*).

all. Geremek would probably be the foreign minister, but then people like my brother Jarosław and Jacek Merkel would also be in the government. We thought that this government would be a re-creation of the unity of the movement.

Undoubtedly Mazowiecki had the most desirable attributes. He satisfied everyone: the Communists, because he was moderate and willing to compromise, a man who had acquired the habit of coexistence over forty years, a slave of his own political schemes; the church, because he was a well-known and practicing Catholic who was willing to make concessions on their part; the Solidarity members, because he was a unionist, an advisor to Lech Wałęsa, the leader of the labor union group at the Round Table; retirees and pensioners, because he was ill, tired, overworked; elderly women, because he had been widowed twice, had to raise his sons alone, was a symbol of fatherly virtue, and so on.

Mazowiecki worked long and hard to develop his political position. But by the time he was named prime minister his position had grown weak. It seemed that Wałęsa pulled him out of a spare suitcase. It was as if he was called back from the exit corridor. He was aware of this. It appeared that in his gratitude to Wałęsa for this unlikely appointment he would show appreciation and repay the favor through loyal, very loyal, cooperation.

Mazowiecki's slowness gave Wałęsa a feeling of security. He knew that he would always be a few steps ahead of the prime minister. He said, "By the time Tadeusz finishes thinking, I would have gotten off five shots."

Mazowiecki is not photogenic and is ineffective on television. He could not possibly threaten Wałęsa, whom Michnik (when they were still on the best of terms—and totally without giving offense) called a "television ape." Mazowiecki talks with effort, gasping into the microphone, as if he were speaking his last words.

The prime minister seemed to be a soft man who in a potentially critical situation would be guided by Lech's advice. This expectation was off.

Reality turned out to be far richer. There was a sociological miracle: Mazowiecki managed to get a chokehold on Wałęsa. The prime ministers's negative qualities turned into assets. His gasping into the microphone was interpreted as an expression of his weariness, which deserved sympathy and understanding. The sad face was taken as a sign of his worry over Poland. The new prime minister mirrored the face of society. He was similarly tired and burdened by troubles and duties. Poles gave him their trust, the trust that they had been saving for the first non-Communist prime minister.

Immediately after his appointment, Mazowiecki informed Wałęsa that he had no intention of being a figurehead. He ignored Wałęsa's recommendations for cabinet-level appointments. He formed the government by himself. The announced meeting of Wałęsa, the Kaczyński brothers, Mazowiecki, and Hall never took place. Mazowiecki ignored Lech's suggestions except in the case of Hall, whom Mazowiecki wanted as well. (It is clear that Lech also proposed Jarosław Kaczyński.)

Leszek Kaczyński: Mazowiecki formed his government as the third political center in Poland, outside of the one formed around the presidium of the OKP ("the family") and the one around Wałęsa ("the court").[5] It was generally agreed that Mazowiecki should have autonomy in picking the personnel for his government (in Wałęsa's opinion, every prime minister must have this kind of freedom). We were not to make the slightest move in attempts to steer the government from Gdańsk. We were discussing this in no uncertain terms, not wishing to duplicate the [Communist] scheme of Politburo-government.[6]

But Lech counted on having more consultations. He thought that the cabinet would become a center for integrating the two political factions—Wałęsa's and Geremek's—which by then were going in different ways while still acknowledging Wałęsa's overall leadership. This does not mean that at the time my brother and I had a concept of the political future for Poland different from the one we have today. We were already thinking about the Center Alliance party[7] and its consequences—I have the ROAD [the Citizens' Movement for Democratic Action], an alternative political party, in mind. But we thought that the conditions for the cabinet in its first months would be more difficult than they actually were. We thought that we needed a government of national unity.

Mazowiecki created a totally autonomous unit; he cut himself off from Wałęsa, and communications between him and Wałęsa became extremely poor. The prime minister, being extremely sensitive, might have thought that Jarosław Kaczyński, as a member of the cabinet, would be a tool to impose Lech's will. Jarosław was only to be a liaison. This situation created tensions that became apparent only a few months later. Wałęsa's hands were tied. There could be no talk about aggressive moves against the first non-Communist government in what was still a Communist country. This would have discredited everyone. That is why the conflict could not begin earlier.

Aleksander Hall: The prime minister saw Wałęsa as a labor leader who was the government's base, a man whose views mattered, with whom good communications had to be maintained. But he also thought that government decisions had to be made by the government and the prime minister. The model in which the center of political power was based outside the government was unacceptable to the prime minister.

As long as there was a Communist party, Wałęsa had to tread lightly around Mazowiecki and his government. He could not attack and weaken his own government. He had to wait patiently for the breakup of the PZPR. It did not take long. The party of leaders like Rakowski and

Leszek Miller (who eventually headed the Social Democratic party) was crumbling before their very eyes.

The Communists needed a guarantee that after all was said and done the pact from the Round Table would still hold. They had established their contacts. First, Jarosław Kaczyński negotiated with them the appointment of Mazowiecki as prime minister. Then on December 20 Wałęsa met Miller in Gdańsk. On December 30 he met Rakowski in the Sejm building. The conversation was held in private.

The workers, especially on the Baltic shore, went mad. Society remembered that just recently Rakowski threatened the shipyard workers, insulting them with gutter language. It was he who tried to close down the shipyard to crush the Solidarity myth. And then the chief of Solidarity meets with this same Rakowski for an hour-long talk, after which they exchange pleasantries ("We'll have to go fishing sometime, Mieczysław").

The sharpest expression of indignation was an open letter from the Solidarity workers' committee at the Kazimierz-Juliusz mine addressed to Lech Wałęsa. Sent by its originators to all the regional Solidarity chapters, it was an attempt at intra-union rebellion.

Lech, meanwhile, recognized his mistake. Society had understood his intentions differently than he had expected. At the rallies (for example, at the J. Piłsudski shipyard) he tried to convince the crowd that he had turned a political somersault, that it was all finesse, and that he, lately a private individual, could call the actual PZPR leader "Mieczysław" while the other replied "Mr. Chairman." He maintained that Rakowski was finished politically and that he "sent him fishing." Not all were convinced by these arguments.

Wałęsa had no way out. To clear himself he had to crush Rakowski. An interview with *Polityka*, a paper where the PZPR leader was boss for many years, was a good occasion. As press spokesman, I purposely set the date of the interview so that the issue would appear the day before the last PZPR congress, January 11. "The new Polish Left must be founded on new, uncompromised people, like [Tadeusz] Fiszbach. The current leaders should remove themselves from political activity for at least a few years," said Wałęsa. Rakowski expressed surprise.

The dissolution of the PZPR was a signal to Wałęsa that he could lay his cards on the table in front of Mazowiecki. Lech still proclaimed support of the prime minister's cabinet but often allowed himself to make critical remarks.

Starting in May 1989, Wałęsa took every opportunity to accuse the Warsaw dissidents of failing to utilize the moment after "L'Internationale" sounded for the last time in the Hall of Congresses in the Palace of Culture and Science. This argument in time became a pillar of his presidential campaign.

Lech Wałęsa after he took control of *Tygodnik Solidarność*, the union newspaper (photograph by Krzysztof Miller, *Gazeta Wyborcza*).

Aleksander Hall: I consider Lech's argument about the government's missing the opportunity to fully exploit the dissolution of the PZPR as purely tactical. If one looks at Wałęsa's activities before the Communist party folded, then I must say honestly (I know the prime minister's opinion and have felt the same way) that Lech made too many gestures toward an alignment with the PZPR: the distasteful meeting with Rakowski, the open championing of Fiszbach, the comments about the left leg [the left-leaning politicians]—then becoming insulted by the results of the gathering [the last meeting of the PZPR] and the strong attack on party property. During that time Wałęsa never said that it was necessary to dissolve the parliament. These comments emerged much later, in summer 1990, when the election campaign was well under way.

Lech did not have to meet Rakowski personally. He could have taken care of the matter through an intermediary or have held the discussion in a private place. The comments in front of the cameras were totally unnecessary.

The Voice of America on December 30, 1989, told us about what was being discussed at Communist party headquarters:

> Rakowski noticed that Lech Wałęsa has distanced himself from prime minister Mazowiecki, because he has seen from the mood of his constituents the dangers to the social and political peace that are brewing as a result of the economic program implemented by Vice–Prime Minister Balcerowicz. Wałęsa also remarked, said Rakowski, that the Mazowiecki government is a transitional government and that he himself thinks that the next government will be headed by Bronisław Geremek.

In my opinion Rakowski did not lie. Lech had made this thought known a few times already. He had to explain the word *transitional* because the remark found its way into the press. A politician of Wałęsa's stature should not spill the beans to just anyone, especially the first secretary of the PZPR and a past prime minister in the Communist government, who in that given moment must have felt some real satisfaction. The reference to the transitional government also appeared in Lech's interview with the Italian magazine *La Stampa* (The press): "This government is transitional by necessity and has my support. But when it makes mistakes, I freely criticize, and this is a success. The next government will have a program, and at its head will no doubt be Professor Geremek." "And then?" asked the interviewer. "If you expect me to say that I will take personal responsibility for the government, then I must answer: I will not exclude that possibility, but I will surely not do it willingly; anyway, please excuse my presumptuousness, but I consider this the final card in a difficult game."

During his inauguration speech in the Sejm on September 12, 1989, Mazowiecki felt ill. Lech watched the broadcast in his own office. When he came out of the office, someone asked, "What would happen if ... ?" He answered, "The next one would be Geremek."

Leszek Kaczyński: I can responsibly say that in the moment when the government was being formed, and after, we did not consider it transitional. Such accusation is unfounded. Of course, we feared that it could fall, but we believed that it would last. The other side, tied to the OKP presidium, kept a distance from the non-Geremek government and in private conversations treated it as one that would not last three months.

On September 27 Wałęsa dismissed Jan Dworak, the chief editor at *Tygodnik Solidarność*, a man who was loyal to Mazowiecki. In his place he appointed Jarosław Kaczyński. The decision was made quickly and executed energetically. It caused a split in the editorial department and a small storm in the journalistic community. There were complaints about the chief's dictatorial practices. Wałęsa assured himself control over the official newspaper of the labor union. The result was another run-in between Mazowiecki and Wałęsa.

On December 12, 1989, Wałęsa pulled from his briefcase a typed description of a legislative proposal that would grant special authority to the government. He called me to his office, gave me the typed pages, and said, "Here, write up the press release and send it out." It was a very serious political item, one that is not written on one's knee. I reviewed the various versions of the release with lawyers, so that I would not make a blunder.

But it turned out that interested parties (that is, the government) learned about Lech's legislative initiative from television. It was a controversial idea, diametrically opposed to the prime minister's philosophy but nevertheless worth some quiet discussion. Wałęsa, knowing Mazowiecki's stubborn streak and the legal principles he represented, should have foreseen that the surprised prime minister would reject it out of hand. To this day I don't know what told him not to discuss the matter with Mazowiecki in advance.

On January 18 Ambassador Vladimir Brovikov, fully accredited representative of the Soviet Union, arrived in Gdańsk. He was to deliver an invitation to Wałęsa for an official visit to the USSR. But before he opened his mouth, Lech said that he had no secrets from the press and that there were many painful matters that must be discussed man to man. "When will you withdraw your armed forces from Poland?" he asked. "It must be done before the end of the year! What about access by Poles to areas that were once part of Poland? When will you explain the events at Katyń, Ostaszków, and Starobielsk?[8] What about reparations to those who were forcibly relocated? Make public the records from the trial of the Sixteen."[9]

Brovikov (a typical specimen of the anti-Gorbachev hard-liner) barely managed to control himself. Lech spoke to the representative of Soviet might in a tone for which all Poles waited, a tone that could never have been used by someone in the government. Mazowiecki learned from the newspapers about this demand for the withdrawal of Soviet troops.

With the formation of the Mazowiecki government, the limelight was turned on Warsaw. Lech was in the shadows. A process of tugging and pulling began. An interview in the *Gazeta Wyborcza* on June 8 started with a statement in which Wałęsa explained the problems connected with his position.

Interviewer: You could have become a representative and then the head of the OKP instead of Geremek, or president instead of Jaruzelski, or prime minister instead of Mazowiecki. Don't you think it would have been better for Poland if you had taken one of these positions?

Wałęsa: I did not give up the game; I merely changed positions. I made Mazowiecki prime minister and Geremek the head of the OKP. They should have no grudge against me that I don't pass them the ball. But they would like me to shout, "Here it comes!" They tell me not to get involved. But I'm in the game whether they like it or not. I may pass the ball badly. Then they should say, "Well done, but there is danger; we must guard against it. Kick the ball right—kick it out of bounds." Instead they are saying, "His passing is no good; he's making a mess because he has no advisors." Sometimes the pass is good; then the receiver kicks it with his foot instead of butting it with his head. Then the viewers boo, not because of my pass but because of his bad kick.

Interviewer: You may pass the ball, but by not being on the playing field you do not play by the rules.

Wałęsa: If they had been good receivers, then there would have been no conflicts. I passed the ball—the withdrawal of Soviet troops. Mazowiecki was not ready. He should have said, "Even Wałęsa says that the troops must go. We know that there are problems with the Germans, that it is difficult, but we recognize that the problem exists." And then everyone would gain. But what did they say?" Stupid remarks. He's causing trouble. Irresponsible." And then we have a conflict, because I then have to answer likewise, "I did not make a bad pass; you did not know how to receive it so that no one would lose."

From the moment that the Mazowiecki government started working, Lech was sincerely involved in supporting it. At the rallies he truly gave his all, but he also harassed Mazowiecki with suggestions that things could be different. In one telex for example, Wałęsa wrote,

Dear Mr. Prime Minister

I must inform you with some sorrow that the broadcast that featured my meeting with the people of the Tri-City area on January 14 at St. Brigid's church was cancelled by a decision made personally by editor Jan Dworak [the onetime *Tygodnik Solidarność* editor].

At this meeting the people supported government policy with an overwhelming majority of votes. The cancellation of the broadcast leads me to believe that the government no longer needs support. I will take it under consideration.

With respect,
Lech Wałęsa

Lacking influence on government policy, Lech led a campaign to support it, at the cost of his own popularity. He assumed the burden of society's dissatisfaction with the slowness of the changes in the army, the security forces, and the police. He took the blame for the impunity of the bureaucracy, the total ineffectiveness of farm policy, the high prices, and everything else. (In time these matters became the cornerstone of his own criticisms.) He tried to explain that the government had great possibilities, that not everything can be fixed at once after forty-five years of abuse. The people gathered around Mazowiecki treated Wałęsa's support as something natural and due them.

Neither side in the conflict between Wałęsa and the government tried to see the viewpoint of the other side. Neither side made a gesture to release some of the tension before emotions triumphed over reason. A statement made later by government spokeswoman Niezabitowska about "the man who would hurry things up with an ax" only added fuel to the fire.

The next misunderstanding between the prime minister and the labor leader was over the idea of speeding up the elections to self-government bodies. An impenetrable barrier arose between them. Lech publicly urged that municipal elections be held sooner. He felt that the tense strike situation in Silesia compelled him to make the statement. A few days earlier he had discussed the matter with the senate marshal, Stelmachowski. Definite dates were mentioned, Wałęsa mentioning the end of March. It is enough to say that the idea matured simultaneously in various power centers. Then Wałęsa met with the prime minister.

Mazowiecki wanted to announce the proposal in his Sejm proclamation. Lech beat him to the punch. Mazowiecki was livid. He accused Lech of disloyalty and the appropriation of other people's ideas (Wałęsa later heard that Niezabitowska spoke about "theft"—but not at a press conference). Wałęsa felt that he was being unjustly castigated. To this day he still feels hurt. And each side sticks by its version of events.

Aleksander Hall: I don't know what it was that Wałęsa discussed with Stelmachowski. I know only that it happened during the visit of the Japanese prime minister to Poland. Prime Minister Mazowiecki was to give an important speech before the Sejm on January 17. He was going to appeal for an earlier date for the election to the self-governments. The plan was known only to his closest associates. He also told Wałęsa, "Lech, at the next Sejm session I will present this idea." Wałęsa approved. I have no doubt as to the truth of this statement. On the following day we received a message from Gdańsk: "I urge the government to speed up elections"—which in my judgment the prime minister correctly interpreted as disloyalty. Mazowiecki felt hurt. I did not get to discuss this subject much with Wałęsa. The explanations Wałęsa gave at the time were not convincing. He simply wanted to show that he was the dynamic element in the situation and a person who had real influence on the government. He did it in a very crude way.

Mazowiecki was further annoyed by Lech's statement to the shipyard workers, that he was "ashamed for the government," which to date could not solve the shipyard's problems. A strike was in the air at the yard, and Lech said that he used those sharp words to get control of the situation.

Leszek Kaczyński: In the spring the social situation grew worse. Lech did not want the potential power that existed in the dissatisfaction to go uncontrolled or to fall under the control of the OPZZ [All-Poland Understanding of Trade Unions] or Solidarność '80.[10] He decided to bear the brunt of the dissatisfaction. Simultaneously, at the beginning of 1990 the problem of Jaruzelski's running for the presidency appeared. We had no clear idea if the other side would support Wałęsa's candidacy. Then Mazowiecki was being put forward as a candidate. It was an attempt to win over Wałęsa, on the condition that he would jettison his closest associates, meaning my brother and me.

At that time there appeared, in the two camps, differing concepts of the future of political life in Poland. I have in mind the idea of forming a Solidarity political party that would monopolize the Polish political scene. I will not link Tadeusz Mazowiecki with this concept, but it is a fact that at the beginning of the year he and his associates, a group popularly called the "cortege," entered into alliance with the "family" (the camps were divided into "family," "cortege," and "court"). At that time Mazowiecki (possibly because of the lack of opposition) attached himself to the unarticulated, but nevertheless very lively, idea on the political scene of a single political group—the Solidarity party.

Aleksander Hall: I am sure this idea did not originate with the government or with the prime minister. I always considered it unrealistic. It was born within the post-KOR elite and was based on the conviction that the unity of the Solidarity camp must be preserved for as long as possible. This idea should not be trivialized, but one should not think that this was to be a monolithic structure.

If Lech Wałęsa thinks that he was responsible for the split in Solidarity in the name of freeing us from the dangers of one-party rule, then he was mistaken. The model of a single Solidarity party was untenable even if Geremek and Michnik had intentions of creating one. The moves by the committees were in different directions, but all went against the existing system. The movement already contained crystallized currents that were driven by the ambitions of individual activists. The divisions were developing naturally and did not have to be hurried along.

Leszek Kaczyński: The formation of the Center Alliance laid waste the plans for the creation of a single party, but it deepened the conflict. The government treated it as a group that was its opposition. Jarosław's frequent public statements that this was not so did not help. The Center Alliance proposed Wałęsa's candidacy for president. At that moment Mazowiecki's candidacy became apparent. On top of the conflict over the concept for the future of Poland was superimposed another conflict, one with personal overtones.

The one important accomplishment completed without Lech's participation was the formation of the Center Alliance—though it was done with his tacit approval. I said that we had a concept (that was in the autumn), but we had no strength to realize it. Lech answered harshly that if we have no strength then we have no concept. I said that in such case we will try to put it into practice ...

On the day that the Center Alliance came into being, the press bureau received a phone request from an evening TV news program for a comment from Lech. I wrote a draft and read it to Wałęsa on the phone. The essence of the comment was that Wałęsa always sought pluralism and therefore greeted with satisfaction every new initiative that would enrich the Polish political scene. He wished the Center Alliance success in its work for the good of Poland.

"Add that I was always a man of the center," Lech told me.

"As a political idea, not as a member," I wanted to be sure.

"Yes."

"But this kind of support is far-reaching."

"No problem."

"I will write that the centrist orientation has always been the one you felt closest to ideologically. How's that?"

"Okay."

When I brought him the completed text, Wałęsa was beaming. He lost the virtue of being a nonaligned leader.

The struggle for influence in the Citizens' Committee (still the most important committee in the Solidarity organization) was a consequence of existing divisions. After obtaining Lech's approval, the new chairman, Najder, decided to expand the committee and nominated twenty-two new people who belonged to political groups not represented in the committee. This included the church.

It was no surprise that this time the chief was crestfallen. He knew that at the meeting on March 31 he would have to legitimize Najder's chairmanship, explain the nomination of the new members, and make some decisive moves against the prime minister, thereby limiting his future options. He would have to approve of the direction in which his policies were going but express dissatisfaction as to the speed of their implementation.

For the first time in my life I was able to observe how Lech prepared himself for playing out such a scenario. He forbade me to book any more interviews. He sat in his office and scribbled on sheet after sheet of yellow paper. Then he reviewed it, even in the car on our way to Warsaw. I expressed my doubt as to the point of these preparations, citing his own remark that he was at his best when "hot and on the march." He let my comment go by.

The car sped along. Because of the rattling, Lech put down his notes and started to read *The Sibylline Oracles*. This was quite an improvement over the usual reading of illustrated magazines or solving crossword puzzles. He was tense, just as before any public meeting. Even routine press conferences bring his nerves and emotions into play. He usually grabs a relaxing nap before departure and later gathers his concentration in the car. We flew on like madmen, unsure of the precise hour of the meeting. Lech, hating to be late, egged the driver on. We got there in plenty of time.

The prime minister, after taking the podium, greeted everyone who supported the government (motioning toward the audience) and those who were giving the government a hard time (motioning toward Wałęsa). Lech's blood began to boil, but he managed to contain his rage. He did not listen to Mazowiecki. He knew that his turn at the podium would be next and formulated his reply. When Mazowiecki finished, Wałęsa rose and took the microphone. He waited as the applause for the prime minister continued. It created the impression of a false start. Wałęsa's anger seemed to grow. Whenever he raised the microphone to his lips, the applause gathered strength. Lech's nerves were beginning to feel strained. The prime minister had appealed to the crowd, asking them not to turn the young democracy into a Polish hell—a hell of argument, backbiting, and conflict. An irritated Lech replied, nearly screaming, that the reforms were going too slowly and that we had gained a victory that we now seemed unable to exploit.

Poland values us, and Poland has no stomach for politics, for political parties. This is the honest truth! We have a beautiful victory; we have tremendous understanding for this government and its great effort. But there is no consummation, my dear people! Why did I ask for special powers for this government? Not because I wanted the government to be above the law. Not because I wanted a nondemocratic government. But, dear people, this is not a time for saving the roses when the forest is going up in flames. When you have a revolution—and we have a revolution—then you have a time of rule by decree! What's going on today? We are so very sentimental. We are so understanding to those who tyrannized us, to those who murdered us, who tried to stifle us by showing us graves! Until today. We are so humanitarian! And what are they doing? Six months have passed and this government still can't resolve the problems at the shipyard! Meanwhile, twenty private companies [founded by former Communists] are doing just fine! On Monday the shipyard will announce a strike to spite Wałęsa and the government! And do you know why? [turning toward Mazowiecki] Because the private companies can get organized [by onetime Communists!] while we are being sentimental! Because we are not issuing decrees! We must immediately stop the wholesale sacking of this country! We must act—democracy, yes—parliament, yes—law, yes—but in an effective direction. Working people get their living from productivity! Today I know that everything we do is correct, but I know that we will not get it done in time. I know this precisely! Of course there is grumbling, hard times—the prime minister said it. Dear people, this is not so! I am the greatest supporter of democracy, and I am for democracy, but I won't live long enough to see it!

Mazowiecki sat petrified, no sign of emotion on his face. There was an embarrassed silence, some weak applause. The corridors started to buzz.

I thought, "The nerves are a bad advisor." Then I started to squeeze my way around the benches to reach Pusz, with whom I wanted to share my observations. Wałęsa also made his way through the chairs on the platform. I did not see him. When I reached my goal there he was as if he had materialized from nowhere.

"How was it?" he asked.

"The nerves are a bad advisor," I answered.

He returned to his seat without a word. I felt stupid.

The prime minister ignored the attack. Immediately after the event, he gave an interview during which he assured all that his relationship with Wałęsa was firm. It had little to do with the truth.

Najder tried to diffuse the conflict. He called Lech on the next day and tried to persuade him to make some kind of a bow toward the prime minister. At a meeting with farmers in Pruszcz Gdański, Wałęsa gave assurances of his support for Mazowiecki and the government. He dispersed the rumors about a conflict. He even added that if had to do it again, he would choose Mazowiecki.

At the next meeting of the committee, May 13, there were many new faces. Lech announced his "return from vacation." Then we heard the quote about "war of everyone with everyone else." Most of the original members of the committee were not among those present. The prime minister was in Kraków. At the meeting of the OKP, Geremek tried to moderate Lech's comments. He pointed out that whatever Wałęsa had to say about the "war at the top," it was done in order to keep peace in the ranks, and even though it caused some jitters, one should still remember that at the Sunday meeting of the Citizens' Committee Wałęsa also spoke about his unwavering support for the Mazowiecki government and parliament. The OKP leader added that Wałęsa himself admitted that his statements are often imprecise but that, until recently, his association with the intellectuals depended on, in the chief's own words, their "kicking these ambiguities into the sidelines." During his last few speeches this cooperation was missing, and this caused the exaggerated level of excitement.

Not two weeks passed since that meeting when Lech was given a chance to restore his prestige. A strike broke out on May 10 in Słupsk, a railway center in the northern railway district. Initially the government ignored it, but toward the end of May 1990, it had taken on worrisome dimensions. The strike started spreading across northern Poland and included Gdańsk. Independent labor leaders Alfred Miodowicz and Marian Jurczyk went to Słupsk.[11] The impasse remained. The government, in spite of a panic in the ministerial offices, kept a calm façade and refused to start talks as long as the strike continued.

On Sunday morning Lech called me and dictated a press release:

To get a true picture of the strike waged by the railway workers, I decided to join it. We reviewed their reasoning. The fact is that the workers have a basis for the strike. But under the present conditions we cannot resolve the strike their way because it runs counter to the reform. Most understood the logical arguments. We started to wrap up the strike. Then three persons entered the stage. One said, "If you end the strike then Czesław, one of the hunger strikers, will immediately commit suicide." Another said, "If you end the strike then Słupsk will continue to strike anyway." Faced with such blackmail, I left Słupsk.

In statements issued by the leader of Solidarity, one can't use logic like that used by the above-mentioned Czesław. Instead, I wrote the following statement: "The strike could have been concluded in a short time had it not been for the position taken by several strikers, who in their stubbornness clung to arguments rejected by most of the others. It is unacceptable that a few fanatically minded persons should dictate to a society that has worked so hard and denied itself so much." I drove over for a consultation on this version of the release. This was the day of the self-government elections. Lech was going to the voting place directly after mass. On the way I handed him the edited text. "You made a mess of it. There's no point in issuing this," he said. A few days later he was still saying how the press spokesman refused to issue a statement on the matter.

Then I understood that Lech was more interested in preserving the faith in his effectiveness than in taking a stand. He was aware that in the public's opinion he was again on target (for the first time in a while). He had been in a slump. He wanted to say that success was near but unattainable, through no fault of his own. I could not write it in the words that he wanted me to use. That would have lowered the statement to the level of an excuse.

But at the time he had behaved in the most logical way: He created a rift in the united and unwavering strike position. The strike committee was willing to accept Wałęsa's proposal on the condition that the participants of the suspended hunger strike would agree. During Wałęsa's twenty-minute visit with the psychologically and physically drained hunger strikers, there was an awful row—the one described in Lech's version of the press release. Lech told us that he rose and in front of the entire group tore up the proposal, which he already had signed, that would have ended the strike.

"I was never here," he said and briskly made for the exit. He told us that he underestimated the strikers. He had thought that after a few moments in which to consider things they would call him at home. They called, but not until that night. The few strikers from the protest committee who were Solidarity members (most strikers were from outside the union), asked Lech to return to Słupsk, assuring him that the atmosphere was favorable. The visit to Słupsk was beginning to produce fruit.

An agreement was signed during the second visit. There was a small controversy: The agreement spoke of ending the strike, while the telex messages the protest committee sent out mentioned only its suspension. But one thing was clear: No one else but Lech Wałęsa extinguished the strike. At the beginning the media reacted spontaneously. Up until 11 a.m. on May 28 the strike was the top news item. Then the enthusiasm died out until the evening TV news, when a teaser preceding the program announced that the railroad strike in Słupsk was over. Viewers then had to wait twenty-four minutes before the report was shown; it was nearly the last item in the program. (It was followed by a human interest story about someone in Łódź who had brought prewar government bonds to a bank and demanded payment.)

This upset me greatly. Throughout the crisis in Słupsk, the TV news had spent the first twenty minutes of every broadcast talking interminably about the strike. The drastic change in their stance toward the strike story could only be attributed to the government's and the broadcast media's bias against Wałęsa. The government's snub was further shown in its failure to call Wałęsa to thank him for defusing the crisis, the most serious since the formation of Mazowiecki's cabinet. There is no excuse for this kind of slight, even if the prime minister and the minister of labor, Kuroń, were both abroad.

It appeared that the fear of the consequences from the strike paralyzed the government to such a degree that it adopted tactics similar to those British Prime Minister Margaret Thatcher might have used. It refused to give an inch. This strike, an illegal one, had to be discredited in the eyes of society, the strikers humbled and isolated. The strategy slowly started to work. Even though a warning strike had been announced, the key stations (Iława, Malbork, Tczew) were functioning. The strike took on a regional character, not spreading to other locations for some time. The strikers needed an accredited leader who would facilitate an honorable end to the strike and could also be a go-between in talks with the government, one who could negotiate a future understanding.

One person who fit those criteria was Wałęsa. The strikers understood this after the failure of the first round of talks. Wałęsa, for his part, needed a spectacular success to stop the wave of critical articles on his anti-intellectual remarks and the "war at the top" rhetoric. His part in resolving a crisis of such proportions would prove that despite declaring war and creating an atmosphere of instability, he was a responsible and serious politician who could help and support the government at a critical moment. That is what happened. Lech gained in popularity and restored the faith of those who had started to doubt his myth. It was one of Lech's biggest successes. But the government saw it in a different light. Although the ending of the Słupsk strike was also a shot in the arm for the new government, Lech's intervention weakened the potency of the shot. Supporters of the Mazowiecki government even accused him of disloyalty by blunting the government's display of force. Lech defended himself by saying that people cannot be pushed to the limits of endurance but must be allowed to see the possibilities and given a chance.

The fact that Lech fails to keep his associates informed does not mean ill will on his part. It is simply his way of doing things—speed, fury, and a large dose of improvisation. When he needs to accomplish something he does not think about others.

Leszek Kaczyński was in the office day and night during the strike action. He knew the matter down to the smallest detail. Involved in the strike from the very beginning, as a representative of Solidarity, he was extremely helpful. But he learned about both of Lech's trips from the radio.

It is hard to describe how mortified I was when I received calls from the domestic and international press asking for details of the talks. Not one of the callers could imagine that I had not been there. I had to give them a version pieced together from the reports of eyewitnesses. I hated to think about what would result from the absence of someone with Lech who would record, in a written document, the statements and agreements he entered into. That is why there was some dispute whether in fact the strike was ended or suspended. I made an appointment for a special discussion with Lech to explain such worries. We talked in the picturesque gazebo in his garden. He was very pleasant; he said I was right. He even added that it was a great error when the press can write about the strike any way it wants to, not as we would want them to write. Those that were absent cannot contribute to setting the facts straight. The next morning he told Pusz, "From today on I do not go anywhere without my press spokesman." There is no better boss than Wałęsa when you can talk with him man to man.

After the strike was settled, Wałęsa's mood improved perceptively. The idyll was short. The strike ended on Monday; Wałęsa sent his letters to Wujec and Michnik on Friday.

The June 15 meeting at the Warsaw residence of the papal nuncio with the Vatican secretary of state Agostino Casaroli was in private. There was some whispering in odd corners that the secretary was to have given Wałęsa a papal reprimand (supposedly in written form). After a forty-five minute conversation, the principals joined the prime minister, prominent members of the Polish clergy (Cardinal Franciszek Macharski, Archbishop Dąbrowski, Bishop Alojzy Orszulik), and the diplomatic corps at a banquet given in an adjoining room. The presence of Mazowiecki was an unpleasant surprise for Wałęsa. Waiters moved among the clusters of guests, serving drinks and fancy sandwiches from silver trays. Pusz, Ambroziak, and Nowina-Konopka labored for over half an hour to bring Mazowiecki and Wałęsa together. Neither wanted to face the other. The whiff of scandal brewing would send all the ambassadors back to their governments with the information that there indeed was a conflict between the two most important men in Poland and it would no doubt lead to destabilization. But one stubbornly took up a position in a corner of the room while the other parked in the grand hallway. Both were doggedly intent on talking to third-level diplomats. Finally, Mazowiecki was dragged toward Wałęsa. Their conversation was short, no more than two sentences: "Well, Lech, have you received my name-day greetings?" "No!" (We later learned that he did receive them, but the card was so ordinary that Wałęsa did not realize that it came from the prime minister.)

After this brief exchange the two politicians turned their backs to each other and continued their previous conversations. "One deserves the other," I thought. Then it hit me that they genuinely could not stand one another.

The situation was saved by the farewell at departure. For a moment the two men froze in a false embrace. The diplomatic corps, pretending to be absorbed in conversation, drank in this ostentatious scene. Everyone seemed to fall silent at once. Insincere gestures are the language of politics.

During the affair Archbishop Dąbrowski and Bishop Orszulik worked on Wałęsa. They tried to persuade him to hold a large meeting like the one at Bishop Gocłowski's residence. Wałęsa consented but on the condition that one of the Kaczyński brothers be among the participants. After this was settled, we left.

On the following day Lech publicly expressed his dismay over the absence of the mention in the press of his sincere and successful meeting with the prime minister. He held this up as an example of media manipulation and the continued hyping of a nonexistent Wałęsa-Mazowiecki feud. I was surprised because Lech knew that the press was not invited into the nuncio's residence, while the two sentences they exchanged during the banquet could hardly be called a political meeting. Furthermore, while giving a statement to the press on his way out of the nuncio's residence, he said nothing about a "successful meeting" with Mazowiecki. If he had wanted the press to take note of the conversation, he would have said something about it.

During the seventy-seventh session of the International Labour Organisation June 14 Aleksander Świejkowski asked both Mazowiecki and Wałęsa the same question: "How is it that Wałęsa, who could sit at the negotiating table with [the much-hated] Kiszczak cannot sit and negotiate with Mazowiecki?" Mazowiecki answered, "I don't believe that he couldn't; we can always call each other and have coffee tomorrow. There is no problem with sitting down at a table. But one cannot sit down at a moment when one is making angry statements at another. I am not angry at anyone." And Wałęsa replied,

> After the incredible speculations that I heard from the Western media I started to wonder what was actually going on. I have no feud with the prime minister; I have no difference of opinion with him. But if there is one, then I will tell the prime minister first and make an announcement that I wish to argue—only then I will call the reporters. But it seems to me that various groups are looking for excuses not to get involved, to make no investments in Poland. That is the main reason. Others are looking for sensation, and all this is bad for Poland. I would like to say that there is no difference of opinion between Lech Wałęsa and prime minister Mazowiecki. Should one arise then we will talk about it first.

Less than a week ago we sat together and talked, a very nice talk between the prime minister and me, but it was not reported. Looks like someone did not care to notice it.

The meeting of the Citizens' Committee on June 24 was conducted in an atmosphere of enmity and arrogance. Many of the original members resigned, among them Bujak, Edelman, Frasyniuk, Geremek, Jan Józef Lipski, Michnik, Stomma, Jerzy Turowicz, Andrzej Wielowieyski, and others. Lech contributed to the negative tone of the proceedings when he asked the graying Turowicz to the front of the room and lectured him ex cathedra, waving at him with his finger. Later he made comments toward Wielowieyski ("Break that thermometer, then you won't register that fever"), and he told Hall that because of his remark that Lech was unfit to be president, there wouldn't be a place for Hall in the next government. These words heated up the atmosphere to such a degree that some epithets were thrown by the opposing side.

Lech then spoke about his conflict with Mazowiecki:

I did not tell you the source of my well-publicized, artificially created conflict with the prime minister. I will skip the first item, that I was accused of stealing the idea about the elections to the self-governments—this is complete nonsense. But it came about in such a ridiculous way that I could have been accused of this. Because I made my statement after a conversation with the prime minister ... I said publicly the things that the prime minister should have announced himself. But I mentioned it myself because there was a threat of a strike in Silesia. I wanted to take the burden off the government, and that is why I said that the lower governmental organs were being blocked. ... I said it, not the prime minister ... and the misunderstanding started.

Now for my conflict with the prime minister when I said that I am ashamed for this government: Look at the context for this statement. It was the fifth strike (you are not even counting them), the fifth strike at the shipyard. At the fourth strike they had put liners into wheelbarrows to get them ready for Wałęsa. At the fifth they had no liners. I had no control over the situation. I had no influence over the dissatisfaction at the shipyard; it appears that no one treats the Lenin [Gdańsk] shipyard kindly. The problem is still unsolved. I was booed, subjected to catcalls. I had to do something to get in control. I said "I am ashamed that the problems of this shipyard, of our heritage, have not been solved to this day." What did I say? Was it such a terrible thing? Did I not have to say it?

This is where the expression *egghead* originated. Because, gentlemen, here we are waging the good fight, and I hear such lies then even a saint could not hold himself back. ... I was only reading the definition as written. ... It is bad that I reached for the book; I'd be better off if I had not read it ... but I did and there it was written—a parliamentary democracy is nothing less than war waged by everyone against everyone else within the limits of ironclad law. I read it. On my return home I hear the government press spokesman say that Wałęsa declared war on the government. The government will not make war on him.

Jesus—Mary! I needed no better gift. And it goes on. "Ax" ... ! Am I such a moron that I would say that the president would actually pick up an ax?! I spoke about decisiveness, accuracy, honesty. That was my "ax." Just the way "Japan" was a metaphor. No, I don't want to eat with chopsticks; but I want an openness to the culture, an openness to development ...

At that time Kissinger, former U.S. secretary of state, was on a visit to Poland. First he came to Gdańsk, then he went to Warsaw for a meeting. When asked about the conflict, he spoke reservedly but understandably, "I must say that the unity between Gdańsk and Warsaw, between the workers and intellectuals, was an inspiration to the world, but especially to Americans. I trust that the current discussion will be resolved by the Poles through the involvement of individuals. Once this is done I think that Gdańsk and Warsaw will again be united and will continue to be led by the work of the intellectuals and inspire the outside world." After his return to the United States, he advised American businesspeople, in very plain words, to hold up their investments in Poland for six months.

Repeated mediation by the church (on July 7 and August 31) yielded no results. Lech announced his candidacy for the presidency. In reply Mazowiecki announced his own intention to seek the office. They never did meet for coffee.

Aleksander Hall: Up until August 31 there was still the chance for an understanding. Until that time the *i* had not yet been dotted. Only after the meeting at the cardinal's residence did the prime minister confront his two options. Either to run for the presidency or knuckle under to Wałęsa. The decision was made at the office on Miodowa Street [the cardinal's residence].

I do not wish to conceal the fact that I was among the enthusiastic supporters of the prime minister's decision to participate in the election. I nursed this idea long before the prime minister adopted it. He thought about it for a long time and took it up with a heavy heart.

Jacek Merkel: Mazowiecki, by saying he did not wish to become a figurehead prime minister, threw away the necessity of standing on a real political foundation, as if he forgot the principles of cause and effect. He forgot that his ascent to office was due to the force of motive power. That motive power was Wałęsa. Mazowiecki was the result because among the people available to Wałęsa, he was the best fit. Of course, Mazowiecki toiled for years over his own position. But it was Wałęsa who created the situation in which Mazowiecki could take over the government. This never entered into the prime minister's consideration. He acted on the basis of the trust that was linked to his person. In this manner he held sway over the Sejm. But as time passed this stratagem ceased to work. When Wałęsa made Mazowiecki prime minister, he tried to convince Mazowiecki that Geremek, Kuroń, Hall, Kaczyński, and even I should be in the government. ... But he did not succeed.

Aleksander Hall: Lech became accustomed to the situation in which he was number one, ... the center of attention and the boss. But the center of power moved away from him; many of his old, close associates became independent while others did not appreciate him. He could not stand it. In the conflict with Mazowiecki Lech's offended ego played a central role.

Krzysztof Wyszkowski: Wałęsa has democratic leanings. This is why he says that he wanted to prevent the creation of a monolithic political party. But every leader prefers a balance rather than a dependence on the one group over which he holds sway. In the moment that a Solidarity political party came into being in which Geremek, Wujec, Michnik, and so on would be the main cadres, Wałęsa would become isolated from society at large and become a puppet. Wałęsa had to build a democracy to assure his own survival. Now he has two parties. He is undoubtedly safer.

During Mazowiecki's year in office, Wałęsa watched as a person he had treated as a tool started to outgrow him politically. Wałęsa's frustration ripened. A man of action who liked constant struggle, a born leader, the victor of many campaigns, he could not find his place within the realities of a democratic nation. He was not able to toil at building a new order. He was not fit for organizational work that was important but unspectacular and out of the limelight.

Mazowiecki showed himself to be a strong personality and won his independence from Wałęsa, but he was not strong enough to lead his government energetically and decisively. His policies were justified and effective for the first six months—up to the moment when the Communists, who still held power (over the army and police), yielded it up. I agree with the view that a radical policy toward the people of the old regime might have caused their military or paramilitary arm to organize itself into an efficient mafia to carry on an underground conspiracy (the example of the Organisation de l' Armée Secrète in France is instructive).[12] The policy of grays and shadows, of small steps and compromise was very good while the Communist regimes that surrounded Poland were still healthy. After they collapsed, there came a time for rapid action without restraint. Mazowiecki was a slave to his own habits. My impression is that Mazowiecki created a plan at the time he formed the government, a plan he started to implement with intensity and stubbornness. But he did not take into account the changes taking place in the Soviet Union and all over Eastern Europe, and the disappearance of the Communists, his counterparts from the Round Table. I'm afraid that under Mazowiecki the reforms would have progressed slowly, as if nothing had shifted on the political scene. Wałęsa has no political hang-ups, whereas Mazowiecki is burdened by the baggage of irrelevant experiences, and this limits him. He is too unsure of himself and too careful.

Did Mazowiecki make a major political and psychological error by cutting himself off from Wałęsa so early and so completely? Would things have gone differently if he had played the game? He knew Wałęsa for years. Did he foresee his frustrations? Did he expect Lech to reconcile himself to the facts? The prime minister's declaration of principles was well founded, but shouldn't he have considered the fact that even before he started governing he already had created a deadly opposition? If he had played Wałęsa's game—which I admit was risky, as it threatened the loss of his own political objectivity—would the split in Solidarity have been so drastic? Moreover, cooperation, though difficult in view of Wałęsa's personality, might have been more effective than activities that kept Wałęsa in the opposition. First, Wałęsa's hands would have been tied. Second, Mazowiecki's sound policies enriched by Wałęsa's political intuition and instinct might have produced excellent results, especially after the dissolution of the PZPR. Third, Mazowiecki would have remained in a political alignment that was analogous to that in which he functioned for many years. He would still have had a stronger partner (formerly it was the Communists) but much better possibilities. Playing off against Wałęsa, he could have used the tactics of small steps and retreats; he could have used his political habits to good effect, but this would no doubt have been more difficult than in the past, as Wałęsa seemed to be a more demanding partner than the Communists. Fourth, if the try at cooperation was not successful, Mazowiecki could have done what he did at the start: say his piece.

Of course he should have accepted Wałęsa's comments more graciously instead of reacting hysterically to every criticism as if it were an attack on the government. Mazowiecki and Wałęsa underestimated each other. Wałęsa undervalued Mazowiecki's endurance and stubbornness; Mazowiecki undervalued Wałęsa's determination. But Wałęsa only knows how to win. That is why on December 9 he became president.

Yes, I am a weak president, therefore you must move up the presidential elections. I thought that I would be good, but I made a mistake; I know I am weak. When you find someone who is better, then I am ready to step down.
—Lech Wałęsa speaking in Gdańsk, at the Fourth National
Solidarity Congress, June 12, 1992

I decided to quit. I could no longer stand to have the public regard me as someone close to Lech who was to a large extent responsible for the things that Lech said and did. I could no longer sustain my faith in Wałęsa. Two months after I submitted my long memo, my dissatisfaction attained critical mass. I knew that I was facing an identity crisis. This was a problem I had expected when I started work for Lech nine months earlier. In addition, after the affair with Wujec and Michnik, I felt a change for the worse in my relationship with Wałęsa. In his mind it all made sense. I know that he reasoned, "Kurski was recommended by Michnik; there is no doubt that he is loyal to him. He is their informer." Wałęsa (you must remember) does not trust anyone, and he did not trust me.

The chief gave me harder and harder assignments. Then he asked me to write two polemical texts: One was to be a rebuttal (a drubbing, as he put it) to Senator Andrzej Szczypiorski's open letter published on June 29, 1990, the other a sharp retort to the telephone opinion poll column that appeared in the *Gazeta Wyborcza*. I was to pick ten of the most critical, spicy, antileftist letters from "real Poles" out of the dozens that arrived in the mail at Wałęsa's office and have them published in the national press or issue them as a press release. Of course, I had to sign both texts.

I refused to do the second assignment. I thought it was foul. I told Lech that these kinds of practices would make both of us look like fools. But I did start working on a reply to Szczypiorski. Writing a good polemic is not a simple matter, and I had no desire to do the job. Szczypiorski's letter was well written. Its more interesting parts are worth repeating.

I see no reason why I should spare you, since you spare neither your longtime friends and associates nor the interests of Poland, which are 100 times more important.

A time has come when someone should stop addressing you as some capricious monarch and treat your position with some seriousness but also with some severity. ...

I believe that you have lost self-control and restraint. From a dedicated leader of Polish democracy you are slowly turning, week by week, month by month, into a destabilizing factor in this nation. The Polish democracy is brittle. The situation in our country is difficult, demanding sacrifices and self-denial from all citizens.

You have said that you want to become the president of our nation. Perhaps you will, and I will regard this as harmful to Poland, because unlike Adam Michnik I do not think that you can be a good head of government just by being faithful to democratic principles. My demands are greater than Michnik's. ...

To assume such a position one must have personal qualities that in my opinion you do not have. First, you are as capricious as a beautiful woman, but those things we may forgive beautiful women we find unacceptable in politicians. Second, you have a contempt for the knowledge and abilities of others, working under the illusion that you know better, solve problems faster, make better decisions. Perhaps sometimes this does happen but no one has a monopoly on infallibility. ...

You do not like educated people. You call them "eggheads." I am an old man and can give you some advice: First think, then speak. A politician who aims high cannot afford to gab like a street peddler! ...

Man is a vain creature, modesty an extremely rare virtue. In addition, circumstances can inflate human vanity and make it the instrument of a person's destruction. If I had experienced the kind of world praise that was given to you for the events that you have unleashed, I would probably not have escaped having my head turned by the conviction that I know more, am wiser, see deeper, and am more correct than anyone around me.

I wrote my answer to Szczypiorski knowing that this would be my last assignment from Lech. My text was not malicious but correct and to the point.

On Monday I went to see Wałęsa in order to tell him that I was going to resign. He was not alone. With him was the previous press spokesman, Piotr Nowina-Konopka. The vise was closing. Wałęsa immediately asked for the reply to Szczypiorski. I read it to him, then handed him a copy. He grimaced with distaste.

"What is this?" he asked. "He is putting it to me, and you only stroke him. They are kicking me, and this one stands there looking," he said to Nowina-Konopka. "You were supposed to hit them back!"

"For you, this would be improper," I answered. Then he saw that his name was at the bottom of the text.

"What? I'm supposed to sign this too?"

Nowina-Konopka tried to convince him that the form of reply I had chosen was the best, better than any other.

"And did you take care of the *Gazeta Wyborcza*?"

"I already told you there is no point ... "

"Then think about it: Do you wish to continue as press spokesman or not?"

"Well, I did want to tell it to you in private but since you have brought up the topic, I resign!"

For a moment there was silence, after which Lech said that it would probably be better this way. I left the office.

I was sitting in my own office when Wałęsa went home. He did not come to the office during the next three days. I then took a long-needed vacation.

The Aftermath

We never talked after that day. I went on to write a book; he went on to become president and occupy the big office in the Belweder Palace. I know he read the book during a flight from Warsaw to Gdańsk. Supposedly he said some uncomplimentary things about it. After all, he did make some obviously angry statements in my direction during an interview on Polish Radio. He said with distaste that the book grew out of the gulf in politics between Gdańsk and Warsaw, that I was young and easily manipulated by Michnik, and so on. I do know, however, that it touched him personally. It struck at the heart of his presidential pride.

I decided to write no more about Wałęsa. I wanted to be free of him. I did not want to become a lifelong expert on Wałęsa, a journalist with one story. That is why this chapter contains mainly the observations of those who accompanied him to the Belweder Palace. I spoke with Merkel, Wyszkowski, the Kaczyńskis, Rybicki, Grzegorz Grzelak, and Jerzy Milewski.

To give Wałęsa's side of the story, I asked for statements from several of his current co-workers: Secretary of State Mieczysław Wachowski, head of the cabinet; Andrzej Drzycimski, the president's press spokesman; Lech Falandysz, legal advisor to the president; and Minister Janusz Ziółkowski, the chief of the president's staff. The first three refused to meet with me, and Minister Ziółkowski was suddenly taken ill.

We Were With the President

Krzysztof Wyszkowski was helping to found the Free Trade Unions in April 1978, which Wałęsa would join shortly thereafter. Together they participated in three strikes. Wyszkowski then went on to become a

Lech Wałęsa is sworn in as president of Poland (photograph by Sławomir Sierzputowski, *Gazeta Wyborcza*).

writer for the *Tygodnik Solidarność*. He supported Wałęsa's bid for the presidency and worked on his campaign staff. In October 1991 he published an illuminating article entitled "Government by the President's Favorites." In one passage he says, "My estimation of Wałęsa was a grave personal error. If I had known the kind of president he would become, I would have not assisted in his election campaign; but this does not mean I would have supported Mazowiecki. I would have distanced myself from the fray."

Jarosław Kaczyński has worked closely with Wałęsa since June 1989 and was the main proponent of his presidency. He filled the role of editor in chief of *Tygodnik Solidarność*, created and led the Center Alliance party, and during 1989–1991 served as a senator in parliament. From December 1990 to November 1991 he was the chief of staff in the president's office, holding the rank of minister. At this time he is a Sejm deputy. He says:

> Even before the appointment of Jaruzelski to the presidency, when I worked in Gdańsk as the secretary of the Solidarity Executive Committee, I already could observe closely Wałęsa's moves toward the presidency. I had no doubts but that it was his direct aim. I wanted

Wałęsa appointed by a national congress for a trial term and not voted in by a general election. This way he would have to serve a short term, then if he proved himself he would have a good chance in the general election. Otherwise, or if he lost the election, then a parliament-cabinet coalition could be set up—headed by a weak president. I always thought that Wałęsa would come to power either through the methods I proposed or at the head of a rebellious populace. The last scenario was unlikely.

Let us imagine a politician of enormous popularity and worldwide fame, who is outside the political structure, saying "If I would govern, things would be better." No establishment could hope to resist him. To me this was obvious at the very beginning. On our political scene Wałęsa was a factor that could not be ignored.

Arkadiusz Rybicki was one of the leaders of the Young Poland movement,[1] a right-of-center opposition group, and its successor organization, the Republican Coalition. During the years 1983 to 1988 he was Wałęsa's secretary. He served on Lech's election campaign staff taking care of press-related matters. In December 1990 he became the president's political advisor. He resigned his position in October 1991. He states:

Wałęsa's political endeavors preceding and following his becoming president must be viewed separately. In the first instance he deserved the appellation of national hero. In the second he is notable for confusion and indecisiveness in handling the power he had won. Wałęsa does not have the basic knowledge of who he is and how a nation functions. When he was seeking the presidency he had no need for this knowledge, but today this is at the core of the problem. The man who would be president must have been the leader of an organization, an organization defined in the strict sense. Solidarity was not such an organization—it was a social movement. Wałęsa was its head, but he was not its boss.

The Polish government has not been strengthened by the fact that Wałęsa became president. Immediately after his election two concepts of the presidency were formulated: the preservation of the existing structure with the necessary personnel changes or the creation of a new structure using the United States as a model. The second plan called for recruiting the very best people to work with the president and the creation of a shadow cabinet. If realized, this plan would place limits on the president's activities; there would be consultations, talks. But he cannot endure routine meetings with people who do not mean much to him at the moment, while the political life goes on nearby.

Grzegorz Grzelak was an associate of Wałęsa during 1980–1981 and after his release from internment at Arłamów.[2] He was one of the leaders in the Young Poland movement, now the Republican Coalition. He was also active in the self-government movement and vice-chairman in the National Mini Sejm of Self-Governments. From February to November of 1991 he served in the president's office as a secretary of state for territorial self-government matters. His opinion:

> Wałęsa's minimum program is to stay on top. But when one is president one should think in relation to one's historical responsibility. Then it is not important whether one stays in power or not, but whether one can lead the country through the difficult structural transformations.

Jarosław Kaczyński: Wałęsa, by becoming president, had a chance to stand at the head of the rebuilding process, to use a coalition rather than merely project a false sense of unity and to create a force for change in Poland, making the changes dynamic. He failed to use this chance. He became involved in machinations based on building up his influence (even with the armed forces) and preserving the old government alignment, as it was in the Communist days.

Krzysztof Wyszkowski: If the president, as commander in chief of the armed forces, is stabilizing and strengthening the old alignment within the army; defending the Communist generals—Piotr Kołodziejczyk and Czesław Wawrzyniak—then this can only mean that he is acting against his own calling.

The slowness with which he is disassembling the political scene is a consequence of his gross failure to understand what makes a nation. "The nation and I," thinks Wałęsa. But to him these two are of different value, where "I" is perhaps valued higher than Poland.

Grzegorz Grzelak: From a historical point of view, this period is one of lost time and will be judged negatively. I fear that we may lose yet another year. I resigned not because Wałęsa ordered me to but because I lost hope that this government could effect the reform which the nation so desperately needs and in which the president should be totally involved. Besides this, I could not reach an understanding with him.

The Bottom Line of the Last Six Months

Krzysztof Wyszkowski: A year and a half has not yielded any positive results.

In the social sector—a great disaster. One would have thought that this was Wałęsa's strong point, an area where he does not have to be educated. But the president failed to unify society and did not inspire it to attain new goals. Even when he did speak about this, it was only empty talk that made impatient even the unsophisticated people, the people who are most sensitive to his rhetoric.

In the economy—less than nothing has been achieved. There is only destabilization, some ideas about reducing prices by 100 percent,[3] the concept of universal privatization with each citizen receiving 100 million zloty, and slogans like "Fix your factories by yourself."

In foreign affairs—no progress, even though the circumstances were favorable. History by itself is carrying us along in a good direction. Today it seems that it is enough to stay with the wave. But reality is different. We will yet have to pay for the idleness, the passivity, and the errors. Wałęsa has achieved nothing; he has not come up with any new ideas. He was always slow to act. On the matter of the Triangular Agreement[4] [Poland-Czechoslovakia-Hungary], he did not take the initiative, though it was evident that this responsibility belonged to Poland. In relations with Lithuania and with Russia and [Boris] Yeltsin there were disappointments. Wałęsa's stance on foreign matters is an embarrassment to Poland. If even Geremek could say that Wałęsa is compromising Polish interests, then it means there is no point in concealing the truth.

In the political sphere—another disaster. The goal should be to stabilize and strengthen the nation. Instead we get Wałęsa's theories about supporting the politically weak (if people get too strong, he cuts them down; if too weak, he props them up), and about "legs." He stated that Polish political life needed a left and a right "leg," that is a political Left and Right. Then he said that we needed more "legs." All this to cover up the consequences—the disorder and the destruction of political scene. His gestures toward the Communists and the OPZZ [Post-Communist labor unions] are part of history, but they were a deviation from fundamental values.

Beginning in July 1982, *Jerzy Milewski* managed the coordinating office of the Solidarity Labor Union Abroad. In February of 1991 he became chief of the National Security Bureau. After Leszek Kaczyński's resignation in November 1991, he took over the position of minister of state for security in the president's office. He states:

Lech Wałęsa, Mieczysław Wachowski, and Andrzej Drzycimski (photograph by Sławomir Sierzputowski, *Gazeta Wyborcza*).

The newspapers may write about a crisis in the president's office, but I see none. I have a positive view of the presidency, even though these are the beginnings. One of the fundamental achievements of this president is to act effectively in order to establish the office as an institution. I am convinced that at the end of the term the stability of the president's office will be most apparent.

Poland needs a person who would be the number-one man, the one who sets direction. The president must be this man. In my opinion Wałęsa is suitable for this post, and I am convinced that for the transition from communism to democracy he is the best president we could possibly have. He should have been elected earlier, immediately after the June parliamentary elections. The selection of Wojciech Jaruzelski was an error that had a damaging effect on the rebirth of democracy.

Jarosław Kaczyński: In the Belweder Palace Wałęsa has created a facility unsuitable for guiding the nation. So far its activities are not leading us directly to disaster, but they do have a negative impact on the president's authority, cause confusion, and offend democratic principle. The president is not using his office to impart a reform-minded direction to governmental activities. He keeps on saying that this is what he wants to do, but these pronouncements are at the level of a foreman directing a crew on a factory floor. The president's basic weakness lies in that he has lost the ability to cooperate with competent people who are well versed in politics. Now we are seeing problems that formerly, thanks to this cooperation, never played a major part. His lack of education and culture is a shadow over his presidency. He gives no moral support, thus instead of becoming a factor to increase the dynamics of restructuring the nation, he becomes a counterproductive force.

Jerzy Milewski: The president must bear the constitutional responsibility for the independence, sovereignty, and security of the nation. He is the commander in chief and the chairman of the national security council [the National Defense Committee]. But unfortunately, the executive's authority is still undefined, and this hinders his ability to take an active approach to his responsibilities. It is a conflict in law. The president is responsible for matters on which his influence is nil. It is not known what he can or should do because it has not been written down. Then when he does take action we hear unfriendly voices raised that he wants to get around parliament and exert influence on the government—things for which he has no authority. But when he does not get involved, then we hear criticism that he has taken a passive stance.

The President's Remoteness

Arkadiusz Rybicki: Not being able to cope with the matters before him, Wałęsa withdrew from the company of people who were politically significant and asked difficult questions, looking critically at his moves. He isolated himself from his advisors because they forced him to exert himself beyond endurance. Wałęsa withdrew into a shell, took on a survivalist attitude, and surrounded himself with yes-men. His loneliness was founded in a sense of defeat. In such a situation the easy thing to do is to tell him that no one understands his plans and that the elite will disappoint. He must have forgotten that he is now the elite of the elite.

Wałęsa's associates could communicate with him only by telephone. He called only when he wanted something. But in order to reach him one had to force a path through a wall of sycophants and protectors. They could say yes, or they could say no. Without knowing politics they created the political reality.

Jerzy Milewski: It was Wałęsa's will not to create a presidential party. Such a party could have been created from the Citizens' Committee movement, should he have wanted it. But he thought, and still maintains, that he should be a leader and a president who is beyond party politics. In this sense he has isolated himself. He does not seek the backing of one group, but wants the support of the majority of the voters. He chose the more difficult road.

The president does not have a set group of advisors with whom he holds regular meetings. This does not mean that he has alienated himself. His contacts with people, with the outside world, are lively and intensive. He often meets with his opponents as well as with his supporters. One need not even mention the meetings with political caucus groups or newspaper editors. This is the Wałęsa style, just as it was when he was the leader of Solidarity.

Grzegorz Grzelak: Wałęsa's strength lay in his ability to cooperate with the people who represented the highest level of politics. Today he is alone. Among the seven or eight main political parties, there is no one who is a confirmed enthusiast for cooperation with Wałęsa. No one thinks that Wałęsa would be a good foundation on which to build the future of Poland. In this sense the president's office is a lost resource.

Jacek Merkel had been Wałęsa's close associate since the time of martial law. He is an efficient organizer and served as the chief of Wałęsa's campaign staff. In December 1990 he became the minister for national security, but in March 1992 he was replaced for reasons still unknown. (The official communiqué from the president's press bureau said something about his being overtired from the huge amount of work. The unofficial rumor—and one not given credence—was that he was involved with a foreign intelligence agency.) At this time he is the president of the Solidarność-Chase Bank.[5] He states:

At the end of the campaign there was a surplus of over 4 billion zloty in the election fund. Both I and Jerzy Kobyliński, my assistant on the campaign staff, thought that the money should be wisely used. We planned to create a foundation—a forge for leadership. Competitive exams would be used as a means to find the very best people. This way the jewels, the very best and promising young talents, would stay in the country. The idea was worked out by sociologists and psychologists working with our staff. We then went to the president in order to present the project and obtain his approval. Wałęsa sat us down in armchairs. But before anyone had a chance to open his lips, he leapt up with the shout "Teleexpress!" [a TV news program]. He turned the TV set on full blast so that, even shouting, I could not be heard above the din from the speaker. His gaze was fixed on the screen; he hardly listened to what we had to say. We accomplished nothing. Jerzy was extremely upset when we left. He was a major contributor to Wałęsa's success, but after this he decided to return to Gdańsk. Later I learned that the president left the disposition of the remaining election fund money to Father Franciszek Cybula, his personal chaplain, who is present at all meetings.

Krzysztof Wyszkowski: Some of Wałęsa's actions are nearly autistic. He is under the impression that he is accomplishing something. He is capable of putting forward concepts that have no basis in reality, for example, the idea of a NATO B and an EC B [East European counterparts to the North Atlantic Treaty Organization and the European Community], which he talked about during his visit to Germany. He has enclosed himself within his own idea of reality. He thinks that others see the aura that he is trying to project, but the aura is invisible and the emperor has no clothes.

Jarosław Kaczyński: Wałęsa suffers from a nearly pathological self-love. The words he uses most often are *I* or *the president*. After a while "I accomplished," "I predicted," "I warned" become unbearable. But I cannot fathom what motivates his public actions—is it self-love or is there something more?

Without a Plan

Arkadiusz Rybicki: Wałęsa could have organized a vast base to support his reforms, but in order to do this one must have a clearly defined goal and a plan for action. One would have to identify the things that are most important for Poland and then work on them in a consistent way. Today even Wałęsa's closest associates would have great difficulty in pointing out the direction in which the president is moving.

Wałęsa did not want to become a "slave" to a plan. He did not believe in planning. Communism fell without a plan; so did the Berlin Wall, he would say. It is difficult to argue with such statements. The fact that leaders like the pope or Prime Minister Thatcher have a plan going several hundred days into the future meant nothing to him. He would say, "God only knows what I'll be doing tomorrow, and I'm supposed to know what I'll be doing in a year?" The lack of an agenda that would cover the work for a few weeks in advance hobbled the government during the time I served in it.

When the press spokesman would explain that the president had ten solutions for every problem, it meant that the president had no solutions at all. Everyone knows that Wałęsa is a man who will not wait when he has ideas, and he tries to implement them before he has a chance to think them over.

Jacek Merkel: Wałęsa had all the information to become the author of several important national undertakings, which would have earned him a place in history. He had support of the electorate, international recognition, his own political camp, plenty of co-workers. Should he have wanted more assistance it would have come—even from the side of his opposition.

Wałęsa is already a historical figure, as leader of Solidarity, and as a Nobel Prize laureate. But he could have taken Poland into the European Community, into NATO. He could have modernized our armed forces. But to do this he needs a scenario for his government's actions and some clearly formulated goals. Wałęsa can't act in concert with a plan, but in a government this ability is essential. He is very good at tactics, at improvisation on a day-to-day basis. In his own judgment he always gets a positive result, with the Virgin Mother guiding him. A president must be a strategist, but Wałęsa's strategy is to apply on-the-spot tactics! This is no way to build up his, or the government's, authority.

Divide and Rule

Arkadiusz Rybicki: The lack of solid goals, inner tension, and an identity crisis threw Wałęsa off balance and made each day into a nightmare. Wałęsa would yell, would throw people out of his office, would not permit anyone to voice an opinion. He could sense that things were beginning to overwhelm him. That is why I believe him when he says now that he would like to quit, that he does not feel in place as president. If one reads between the lines of the statements he gives to the press, one can see this nightmare in the words he utters, that the last few months were the worst period in his life. "I don't want to, but I must," the words which he often repeats, reflect the true inner conflict.

Jacek Merkel: In the Belweder Palace there is the conviction that the instrument for exercising authority is the so-called in. If someone has an "in" with someone else, then he can rule. Those with the most "ins" have the most authority. This principle is universal, so everyone wants to have an "in" with Wałęsa as well.

I do not know, and I don't want to know, why Wałęsa made it impossible for me to work with him by giving me a series of absurd assignments. His accusation òf disloyalty on my part was a reaction to my refusal to act without a clearly formulated plan intended to build a government. All he wanted was to be rid of me. But aside from my own situation, the principle of removing competent and loyal people is worrisome.

Jerzy Milewski: A few months after Merkel's removal, the president asked him to be a candidate for the civilian position of defense minister. Merkel turned it down because he was already bound by his contract to be president of Solidarność-Chase Bank. If the president had had some doubts about Merkel, then he would not have asked him to take the position.

Krzysztof Wyszkowski: Those who know Wałęsa know how liberally he treats the nation's interests. His punctuality is merely a cover for his idleness. Wałęsa is always saying how tired he is, that he's working at 1,000 percent over quota, and so forth. This is an attempt to blur matters. The Belweder is shut tight, and he can successfully hide the fact that nothing is getting done, that the apparent activity is only for show. For example, the recent ideas about creating NATO B and EC B are merely canards to cover up the total emptiness. There is a price to be paid for such doings; they cannot be concealed with talk.

Grzegorz Grzelak: Without a doubt Poland's political successes are also Wałęsa's personal successes. In his case his personal interests are interwoven with the public interest, and it is hard to tell which is uppermost. I cannot believe that he would be satisfied with placing himself in a favorable position at the expense of the country.

Jarosław Kaczyński: Wałęsa showed a lack of determination in the struggle for speeding up the elections and implementing a good set of election laws. We [the Kaczyński brothers] had to fight with him over this matter, which had to be brought to an eventual conclusion—even if it led to the dissolution of parliament. This might be the result if the parliament tries to enact a set of nonsensical election laws.[6]

Leszek Kaczyński was Wałęsa's close associate since the latter's release from Arłamów. He served as the vice-chairman of Solidarity, and was popularly called the brain of the union. During 1988–1991 he served as a senator in parliament. He succeeded Merkel as minister of security in the office of the president, leaving the post in November 1991. He states:

My brother and I had a concept according to which Solidarity would split into two opposing political blocs. Wałęsa supported this idea, saying that it was necessary to have a right and a left leg. We formed the Center Alliance which caused ROAD to spring into existence.

But Wałęsa was not through yet. He yelled for a third, fourth, seventh leg—at which time we came to the conclusion that he wanted to totally fragment the political scene because that would benefit him. Wałęsa was a faithful partner to our concept for only six weeks. Then he tried to make sure that the Center Alliance would never become a political power. In the middle of 1990, about twenty local citizens' committees wanted to join the Center Alliance, but he blocked the initiative.

But this is characteristic of Wałęsa. Jarek [brother Jarosław Kaczyński] was moving ahead but was not in any way a political threat to Wałęsa. But Lech sees an opponent in anyone who attains an independent position.

Krzysztof Wyszkowski: Wałęsa is burdened by the tremendous responsibility of working toward the common good, but he has the tendency to gather about him people who embody pragmatism, cynicism, and vileness—all the things opposed to good. He is supposed to be a charismatic leader, intent on realizing ideas, but he is also a psychological being, a man who wants to assure his own material interests. Someone must obtain money for him. He must then surround himself with loyal people—people totally committed to him—loyal because without him they are nothing. These people may not be from the political scene or people who could betray him somehow. They must be true and devoted slaves who draw benefit from their closeness to the president. This mechanism causes the accumulation of individuals with little morality and creates a corrupt atmosphere around the president. But for Wałęsa, having such a support system is a psychological need.

Jarosław Kaczyński: I did not have daily contact with the president. After taking care of my business, I would leave, even though he wanted to draw me into his court. He wanted me to have my office in the Belweder. I had no such desire.

The Court and Its Carousel

Jacek Merkel: If one does not wish to make decisions, then one should bring in competent associates and officials who may formulate the appropriate solutions and prepare the necessary documents for signature. Otherwise it all becomes the kind of farce I was privy to when Jerzy Milewski was nominated for the position of national defense minister.

This happened just before the Kaczyński brothers and Maciej Zalewski handed in their resignations from the president's office. Jerzy Milewski was called to the Belweder. Among the people receiving him was Mieczysław Wachowski, who presented him with a document that stated that he would be assuming the responsibilities previously held by Leszek Kaczyński. Milewski asked, "What about the secretary of KOK [National Defense Committee]?" Wachowski seemed to know nothing about any secretary or KOK. Milewski then gave a short lecture on the law, the constitution, procedure, the presidency, and the secretary of KOK. Wachowski then asked who the secretary of KOK was. Milewski again gave a lecture but this time on recent history: First it was some Communist general, then Merkel, after him Zalewski, but no one saw him get the appointment. "Well, was he, or wasn't he? Doesn't anyone know?!" shouted Wachowski, swelling with anger. Wałęsa was waiting in his office, also boiling with anger, for it was Friday afternoon. He wanted to leave for [his home in] Gdańsk, and the crew was already warming up the plane's engines at the airport. Wachowski grabbed the phone to call the president's office. "Was Zalewski appointed?" No one knew. A search for Zalewski was launched. A car was sent. Meanwhile time was being wasted. Zalewski was nowhere to be found. Wałęsa was getting angrier and angrier. Finally Zalewski was found. He stated that he was the Secretary of KOK. Quickly the documents were composed. One fired, the other hired! Wałęsa signed and breezed off for the airport. The Polish state finally had a KOK secretary.

Jarosław Kaczyński: Wachowski came to me, asking if I would arrange for him and Drzycimski to receive secretary of state rank. He said that he wanted me to do it so "that there would be peace between us," but at the same time he threatened to get it done with or without my help. I went to Wałęsa to express my disapproval. Wałęsa said, "You must be joking, secretary of state rank for them?" But after a few months both had it.

Wałęsa has a terrible appraisal of human motivation. He believes that all those around him want perquisites and positions. This leads to

Mieczysław Wachowski, the chief of the president's cabinet (photograph by Kuba Atys, *Gazeta Wyborcza*).

some comic situations. If he wishes to punish someone then he will threaten the miscreant, "You won't get anything for six months." Wałęsa knows that under today's circumstances six months is eternity. But he does not realize that there are people whose motivations in life are governed by other factors.

The World of the Valet

Jarosław Kaczyński: Today my evaluation of the presidency is most critical. I expected that things would not be well, but I never expected them to be this bad. I never expected someone like Mieczysław Wachowski to show up.

Mieczysław Wachowski became Wałęsa's driver in 1980, thanks to a recommendation by a certain Catholic family. He quickly became Wałęsa's friend, then his trusted confidant, majordomo, and organizer of free time. During martial law he was arrested but released after one day. He assisted the Wałęsa family until 1983. Then, suddenly, he broke his contact with the Wałęsas. During 1983 to 1989 he started his own business, a tire retreading shop. In 1989 he went on a trip around the world as a boatswain on the sailing ship *Zawisza Czarny*. He returned to Gdynia in April 1990. Two months before Wałęsa took the presidency

Wachowski showed up in his office. After two weeks Wachowski supplanted Pusz, Wałęsa's personal secretary. He fired two dedicated secretaries. After Lech's election to the presidency, he become the cabinet chief of staff, the number-two man in the nation. At the Belweder he ostentatiously paraded around with a list of persons to be fired. Today, not one of those people is employed by the president.

Leszek Kaczyński: Wachowski is an influential man, and his role in the government is enormous. He is dangerous and capable of anything. His presence in the Belweder is an insult to the government. He tries to gain influence, entrap others in a net of invisible alliances, and twist himself into matters of government that he considers important. His evaluation of what is relatively important is never wrong; this includes the armed forces, special services, and policy toward Russia. Recently banking was added to his list.

Jarosław Kaczyński: I will not disagree that it would be difficult to demonstrate that Wachowski is a serious threat to the state. Some information, however, must be taken on faith. Wachowski is a secret person. I will refer chiefly to events where witnesses were present: the matter of crossing out portions of Wałęsa's speech in Brussels and Admiral Kołodziejczyk's frequent visits to Wachowski's office. That Wachowski plays a dangerous role—that this is a person who is nearly unknown, has a strange resume, and has no preparation or merit for the political part he plays—cannot be perceived by a person who has not spent time in the Belweder. Yet the fact that he is a secretary of state and one of the most influential people in the country is no less strange.

The gravest accusations were made against Wachowski but 100 percent proof has not been found. There is some circumstantial evidence given by his resume, especially since he made his appearance at Wałęsa's side in 1980, and various character traits. There were also signals given by other governments. I will speak now about facts not yet revealed to the public.

Wachowski is at the center of an invisible alignment in the military and the special services. He has a relationship as well with General [Edward] Weinert, the chief of the Vistula unit of the KBW [Internal Security Corps] for whom he tried to get an appointment as the minister for internal security. It's well known that the KBW corps was the old regime's last barricade. Its officers were picked even more carefully than those in the security service. It was a given that the security forces might collapse and then the KBW would have to take on the rebellious populace and the mutinous army.

Weinert is a general who was part of the old Communist arrangement. He often came to see Wachowski, who then would defend him
like a lion before Wałęsa and me. When he tried to get the ministerial
post for Weinert, questioning at every opportunity Minister [Henryk]
Majewski's qualifications, it all started to make sense. Weinert would
become the second Communist minister, after Kołodziejczyk, whose
appointment depended on Wachowski. Fortunately, all his efforts
failed.

Often when I would go to the Belweder I would see a distinctive
coat and hat with an admiral's insignia. I had no doubt that these
belonged to Minister Kołodziejczyk. After all, we don't have many
admirals. I first thought that he was visiting Wałęsa, whom I was also
coming to see, and feared that his presence would interfere with my
seeing the president. But after a few times I caught on that Kołodziejczyk was in Wachowski's office.

For a long time Wachowski manipulated Wałęsa so that he would
go against the idea of a Triangular Agreement, but more specifically
against Vaclav Havel and Jozsef Antall, the Hungarian prime minister.
Then Wachowski suddenly changed his mind. First I thought that
Wałęsa had changed his own mind, but later I learned that it was
because of Wachowski's influence.

To state it briefly, Wachowski has a very negative influence on
matters that are essential to the nation. Worse yet, this is not the result
of simplicity or a lack of education. There is a logic visible in it, and
this leaves me with some serious suspicions. If I had to deduce from
Wachowski's actions his purpose and goals, I would have to say that
he aims to preserve the old Communist influence in the government
and impede any policies that would take us closer or strengthen our
ties to the West.

Arkadiusz Rybicki: Wachowski knows how to speak the language of
the old establishment. He knows the veiled threats and phrases that
make the old apparatchiks sit up and take notice. "The government in
Poland is the president, and the will of the president is ... well, you
know, understand," he says.

Leszek Kaczyński: Wachowski used the method of weeding out
Wałęsa's old associates. First to be fired was Krzysztof Pusz, then
Arkadiusz Rybicki. As for me and my brother, to us he repeatedly
proposed alliances that we rejected. Anyway, he does not keep agreements. He did not hide the fact that it was he who would decide who
would stay in and who would depart from the president's office. He
would often call upon the "will of the president," even though no

express command was given. He showed an uncommon self-confidence.

The very phenomenon of his career is puzzling to me. He returned after seven years in November 1990, and in a few weeks he became Wałęsa's number-one man. He is in constant contact with Wałęsa and has contact with his family as well. I think that his demonstrative loyalty and uncritical submission satisfy Wałęsa's psychological needs.

These are things known in the president's office, but they are extremely difficult to prove. In one instance Krzysztof Pusz was able to catch Wachowski when he tricked an individual into giving him $3,000. But the president made Wachowski return the money and the matter ended there.

Jerzy Milewski: I don't know what the basis is for the supposed pathological influence exuded by Minister Wachowski that Jarosław Kaczyński is talking about. I never saw anything like it. Secretary of State Wachowski is the chief of staff in the president's cabinet. He organizes the president's work. It is a very important, difficult, and thankless function. In the United States this job is performed by the White House chief of staff, who does not actually govern but is one of the most influential men in the presidential circle. Wachowski plays a major part, but the conjecture that Wałęsa is in some way controlled or steered by his chief of staff is unfounded. No one has been able to do this. President Wałęsa cannot be manipulated.

Krzysztof Wyszkowski: Wachowski is not enlightened by any historically motivated goals. The ambition of politicians is to be remembered favorably in the history of their nation, but for him the only purpose for involvement in government is amusement, a lark. Here is someone without a past, who has never done anything for his country, who suddenly becomes the number-two man in government. He is even received by the British queen. And it turns out that history is trash, that it can be ridden like an old mare, spit upon, kicked, but it still stays compliant. The fact that Wachowski can decide the fate of a people as proud as the Poles is a mockery of history. But this confirms Wachowski's view of the world.

A Dark Reflection of the President's Soul

Krzysztof Wyszkowski: Around Wałęsa, Wachowski creates an atmosphere of contemptuous, cynical, and venomous humor at the expense of the national interest and government institutions. This is a reaction to the psychological tension. Some get drunk, others curse, still others lock themselves in bathrooms and scream. Wachowski relieves Wałęsa with a massive, vulgarly delivered dose of contempt for the world, a dose colored with humor and feverish, nearly diseased hilarity. If Wałęsa had been more cultured by nature he would not be able to endure it. Wachowski is nothing more than Wałęsa's own dark side. He does not have two faces. His face is totally unknown.

Jarosław Kaczyński: I can only explain Wachowski's bewildering career with the opinion that he satisfies Wałęsa's various needs, but especially his psychological needs. Perhaps he has something on Wałęsa? I do not know. Wachowski himself has said that Wałęsa throws him out four times a day, that he practically wipes the floor with him. And yet his word counts with Wałęsa. Wachowski is quick and intelligent. He has cleverness, a criminal's cleverness, always ready to do anything to satisfy the president. Many times during my conversations with Wałęsa I brought up the matter of Wachowski. It was the bone of contention in our disagreement. When I asked for his ouster, Wałęsa's answer was an evasion.

Krzysztof Wyszkowski: Wachowski is always in the presence of the president, but he does not exist as a public persona, gives no interviews, and explains himself to no one. This is the way he is supposed to be: invisible. His job is to take care of the shadowy matters. But to put things pragmatically, these matters don't need to be so shadowy. Many things could be revealed and allowed for, for example, that money is necessary and the president must gather it somehow.

Hour of Trial: The Moscow Coup of August 1991

Leszek Kaczyński: I learned about the coup in Moscow in the morning. I immediately went to the office and called the president, but he informed me that he had already talked with those who mattered and that my help was not necessary. I was not invited to the Belweder. At that time I decided to resign my position as minister of national security, but for various reasons did not hand in my resignation until just before the elections.

Jarosław Kaczyński: During that time my brother and I were seeking guarantees from NATO. It seemed that this coup was an opportunity to accomplish this, but our effort failed. Wałęsa rejected an interesting offer for meditating this matter. In addition, to our surprise, he refused to call a meeting of the National Defense Committee. He concluded that he needed no advice.

The Moscow coup marked the beginning of decreased contact with Wałęsa. I stopped going to the Belweder. I had already prepared my resignation, and it had been resting in my desk drawer since spring. Just like my brother I waited to submit it until right before the elections, fearing an attack by the press that we were "thrown out" because of Telegraf affair.[7]

Leszek Kaczyński: During the coup I decided to act through frequent contact with the prime minister. Bielecki had created a special staff on the ministerial level. In addition to assessing the entire situation, they evaluated the danger to our eastern border, not so much from the Red Army as from refugees. I tried to follow NATO's reaction in relation to Poland and other East European countries. I thought that this might be a chance to obtain some guarantees from the North Atlantic Treaty Organization. The information coming in from the West gave this possibility some hope. It all played itself out within forty-eight hours, and everyone had a good idea of the enormity of the events and the scale of danger.

On August 19 I put in an official request for a meeting of the National Defense Committee, but by the afternoon I knew it was to no avail. Lech said that he was "like a fish in the water and would take care of everything" and that Minister Wachowski was assisting him. It was obvious that he concluded that this was a matter only he was qualified to handle.

Jerzy Milewski: The president did not call a meeting of the security council probably because he did not think that it could help him or the government in the jobs each had to do. After all, each of the members has the right to initiate a meeting, but no one from the government requested it—not the foreign minister, the defense minister, the internal security minister, nor the prime minister. The president conferred with members of the council singly or in small groups but never with the full council. They met at the Belweder, not in the BBN [National Security Bureau] headquarters at 5 Aleje Ujazdowskie.

Jacek Merkel: The president did not call a meeting of the National Defense Committee, the very body created just for such a contingency. Instead, he said, he called together a small, not constitutionally mandated, body of uncertain composition. Possibly the members included Minister Drzycimski, Minister Wachowski, and the chaplain —Father Alfred Franciszek Cybula.

Jerzy Milewski: The prime minister created a multidepartmental crisis board. During the days of the coup the presence of 45,000 Soviet troops in Poland became a major problem. From a strategic point of view the number was small but sufficiently large to create a provocation of some kind.

Leszek Kaczyński: Both my brother and I tried to pressure Wałęsa to put off the start of the next round of negotiations on the removal of the Soviet troops. One reason was that Ambassador [Yuri] Kaszlev [of the Soviet embassy], who was asked to come to the MSZ [Foreign Ministry], concluded that the new government should be treated as the permanent ruling body, while our own sources indicated that the coup was falling apart. The Russian side did not know whom it was representing. The MSZ wanted the talks to go ahead, and they did, yielding no progress.

Jerzy Milewski: I was the chief of the National Security Bureau and the vice-minister for national security. The BBN has no executive authority; it has no police or army units under its command. It only collects and analyzes data for use by the president and the security council and formulates proposals. We worked around the clock and waited for developments.

Jacek Merkel: If the government of a neighboring country is suddenly seized through a military coup, such an act threatening the safety and sovereignty of Poland, then the government machinery should go into action according to a secret, previously worked-out plan. The president should immediately call for a meeting of the National Defense Committee at which the ministers of defense, foreign affairs, and internal security would report on the matter. A staff should be created to deal with the crisis. On the basis of constitutional authority, a special meeting of the government should be convened. During this time the president's press spokesman should be able to work out the presidential proclamation.

The president as commander in chief of the Polish armed forces had the responsibility to appear on television with a patriotic proclamation, one similar to that given by President John Kennedy during the Cuban missile crisis. This is how history is built. Such a speech would have entered the canon of important Polish proclamations. Meanwhile, it was Drzycimski [the president's press spokesman] who, wooden-faced, read some kind of text. This is not what the nation expects in a dramatic moment such as this.

President Lech Wałęsa behind a police cordon (photograph by Sławomir Sierzputowski, *Gazeta Wyborcza*).

Instead, there was surprise, helplessness, fear for one's safety (I heard that Wałęsa asked for more security), and nervous phone calls to Kiszczak and Jaruzelski [ex-Communist generals]. This is how the president behaved in the first hours of the coup. If he called Jaruzelski, who would have some influence among the potential victors in the coup, then this must have meant that he had no faith in control over his own army. This is not how the head of an independent nation should behave.

Krzysztof Wyszkowski: Wałęsa was encouraged to make a speech on television. But he could not decide, did not want to; finally, he refused. The necessity for a public appearance by the nation's leaders in the moment of potential crisis was so obvious that Prime Minister Bielecki decided to go in front of the cameras. He had prepared a text for a speech, but Wałęsa forbade the broadcast.

Jarosław Kaczyński: Wałęsa must have been convinced that the coup would succeed, but from President Bush's speech it seemed that it was falling apart. Bush would not have casually taken the matter to the edge and provoked a confrontation with an entrenched government that had 30,000 nuclear warheads at its disposal. But already on Monday afternoon he took an extremely tough stance.

At the last moment Wałęsa ignored Boris Yeltsin, betting on Mikhail Gorbachev. I believe that this was because of his political infantilism and lack of independent judgment. I don't know whether it was the press or other sources that influenced him to say, "That Yeltsin is a satrap."

A good while before the coup, intermediaries had suggested a spectacular meeting between Wałęsa and Yeltsin during the pope's visit. This could have lead to a reconciliation between the Polish and Russian peoples. Such a message would have been far-reaching. I do not know if it could have been done. There were other proposals as well.

Leszek Kaczyński: The coup fell apart. The staff spent a few days considering the relationship between Gorbachev and Yeltsin. Everyone thought that the first was finished. That is why the Belweder's stance to stick with Gorbachev was hard to understand. I know about the much-delayed call to Yeltsin. My brother was pushing for this. The delay was supposedly caused by technical difficulties. I do not know the truth of it. Others managed to get through.

Jerzy Milewski: The president did call Yeltsin and received the latter's thanks for it. Because of interrupted service and the great number of the world's leaders trying to get through, the call from the Belweder got through very late. We could not reach Gorbachev at all. Bush and Mitterrand did get through, but other leaders also had no success.

Jacek Merkel: I cannot understand Wałęsa's behavior. It cannot be explained, and there is no way to justify it. I am also opposed to the way Wałęsa represented Poland while making his phone call to President Yeltsin. When finally, as one of the last European leaders, he managed to get through to the Russian president, the eyes of millions of television viewers beheld a sweating Wałęsa with rolled up sleeves and a loosened tie. He had a newspaper spread out on the desk before him while Wachowski hovered behind his chair, slipping him some "extremely urgent" papers to sign. Even the most basic courtesy, including to one's fellow citizens, requires that a transmitted conversation of this importance should have at least the minimum setting it deserves.

Jerzy Milewski: The president tried to make telephone contact with Boris Yeltsin, Mikhail Gorbachev, and Gennadi Yanayev [the leader of the coup]. I was not present at the discussions on this subject. As far as I know, the prevalent view was that the seizure of power by hard-line Communists, the army, and the KGB would be a serious threat to our sovereignty. Reasons of state required action with extreme care. It was determined that we should not give Yanayev any cause to make a case that the Polish government was acting against him.

The president did not speak with Yanayev. I do not know if a letter was sent. I was not among those who made the decisions. I saw no letter nor the draft of one. Had I been involved in drafting such a text, I would have opted to include the following points: We are an independent nation and intend to stay that way; we have no claims against the USSR; we expect a quick end to negotiations and the withdrawal of the Soviet troops from Poland; the agreements concerning the deliveries of oil and natural gas [into Poland] will not be broken. This letter would not in any way have legitimized Yanayev. It would have provided a certain amount of political cover against any possible attempt by the coup participants to restore the Soviet empire after they were firmly implanted. I do not believe that any letter was sent. Fortunately, the coup fell apart quickly, and there were no communications with Yanayev. After all that, it was really unnecessary, as the coup participants had no time to think about Poland.

Jarosław Kaczyński: I know that while the coup was on a letter was written; in it President Wałęsa gave recognition to President Gennadi Yanayev. I can only guess that the letter's author was among Wałęsa's closest associates.

Wałęsa had said, "I know Yanayev." [In this sense] my brother also knows him; he met him in Geneva along with Wałęsa, where Yanayev was representing Soviet workers. Later in Prague, during the meeting that put an end to the Warsaw Pact, Leszek was walking down the corridor when Yanayev, the head of the Soviet delegation, accosted him with "Ah, comrade Kaczyński!"

Jacek Merkel: Well-informed sources at the Belweder tell me that Wałęsa had a letter to Yanayev ready. He would have sent it, but it was heroically blocked at the last moment by prime minister Bielecki. Had the letter gone out, Wałęsa would have joined the likes of Muammar Qaddafi, Saddam Hussein, and Stanisław Tymiński.

Leszek Kaczyński: On August 19 I learned about the decision to send a letter to Yanayev. I don't know whose idea it was; it might have been the president's or Wachowski's. This was after the affair connected with the crossing out of certain parts of Wałęsa's speech that was given at the Brussels NATO headquarters.

The Gray Eminence

Leszek Kaczyński: At first there were two versions of the Brussels NATO speech. One came from the Foreign Ministry; the second was enriched with fragments added by the president's office. I had two meetings with [Foreign] Minister [Krzysztof] Skubiszewski, and we finally settled on a compromise version that was given to Wałęsa and a copy sent to NATO. But in Brussels I learned that there was confusion in the Polish delegation about two versions of the speech. I explained that there was only one—the one we had agreed on with the Foreign Ministry. But the people in Wałęsa's circle kept pretending that they did not understand. We went over it three times. I kept repeating, "There is no other version!" At the residence where the Belgians housed their official guests, Wachowski read the speech and declared, "There will be no anti-Russian provocations!" On the next day I was to go to NATO headquarters with the president, but Wachowski, speech in hand, pushed himself into Wałęsa's car ahead of me. It was then I noticed that a number of sentences in the speech, had been crossed out. Wałęsa gave the speech, and it turned out that it was a shortened version.

The part that Wachowski crossed out is as follows:

> We cannot, however, hide the truth [about Polish-Soviet relations]. There are problems that cast a shadow over our cooperation. Even though we have tried to be flexible in the negotiations, there still is no movement on the withdrawal of the Soviet troops stationed in Poland. The USSR has proposed dates that fall far in the future and an extremely slow tempo for the withdrawal of these units. Such policy toward a sovereign Poland is not tolerable. We are waiting for a positive breakthrough that will improve the atmosphere for peace on the entire continent.

Jerzy Milewski: I believe that if Wachowski crossed out a portion of the president's speech, it was because he was requested to do so. I was not in Brussels during this visit, but I know Wałęsa well enough to be sure of this. After all, the text of the speech given to journalists contained that paragraph, therefore the president was not concerned with its deletion but with the way it would sound when delivered.

Leszek Kaczyński: At the Belweder I was not able to shape the president's defense policy, but I was still powerful enough to block some bad ideas and unfortunate appointments to the rank of general. A few days before August 19, I went against personnel changes in the command of the armed forces special services. I knew that one of the people involved in Wachowski's invisible alliances would be coming up for appointment. On the day of the coup I learned that the appointment was confirmed [a reference to Czesław Wawrzyniak, the chief of the army special forces]. I think that Minister Wachowski, with some premeditation, brought the appointment up for signature at a moment when the president felt that a threat existed.

Jarosław Kaczyński: It is not difficult to imagine what would have happened had Yanayev succeeded. In practical terms it would have meant the loss of control over the things that are important now. It is clear that at that moment the old Communist contacts would have regained their former strength. The fact that men like Admiral Kołodziejczyk have been given entrée to influence would bring Wałęsa to the threshold of unacceptable decisions.

Banker's Poker

Jacek Merkel: It is obvious that there are many, far better qualified candidates for the position of president of the NBP [Polish National Bank] than Mrs. Gronkiewicz-Waltz. Krzysztof Bielecki, Leszek Balcerowicz, Marek Dąbrowski—all have administrative experience and are economists. The first two are well known in the financial world. They have conducted negotiations with foreign nations, an important qualification for a National Bank president in view of the Polish debt. My estimate of Gronkiewicz-Waltz's qualifications is low. She has a specific method of perceiving the national financial system through the necessity of battling fraud rather than steering this intricately delicate system. She is the coauthor of the presidential veto to a move blocking her appointment. She is the leader of the Victoria political party, whose entire program is centered on supporting Wałęsa. (In the last election the party received about 1,000 votes.)

Leszek Kaczyński: The choice of Gronkiewicz-Waltz as president of the NBP fits into Minister Wachowski's logic. No one questions her qualifications in the area of bank law, which is all that is necessary to be an advisor. She is a good professional, but this is not enough to become the president of a bank that employs 9,000 people and controls the entire national financial system. I know that she has received recommendations from the Belweder that have nothing to do with the bank's financial policy.

I fear that with the mystical connection between the new bank president and the nation's president the method for administering the bank will depend on telephone calls from Minister Wachowski and his actions in the "will of the president." A work style based on telephone calls could mean a bad ending for the bank and for its lady president, who after all said that the president has an exceptional instinct for the law. I will not deny that Wałęsa has an incredible political instinct, but he has no instinct for law. He does not understand the concept of law at all.

Jacek Merkel: The most worrisome is the mechanism of political action Wałęsa is using, though he is using it effectively. As a top-class tactician he did a surprising thing. He humiliated and ridiculed the Sejm, opening up the possibility of appointing a prime minister in the same way as he did the NBP president—by way of repeatedly proposing the same candidate who was previously rejected by the Sejm. In the face of a three-month limit, the president will hold his own and force his candidate through or use his constitutional power to dissolve parliament. But after the experience with Gronkiewicz-Waltz, Wałęsa knows that the Sejm will bend to his political dictates rather than allow itself to be dissolved.

What Next?

Jacek Merkel: At one of the final National Defense Committee meetings the subject under discussion was defense doctrine. I had heard that the president did not wish to familiarize himself with this topic. I think that in the long term Wałęsa will not be able to maintain his exclusive position whereby he can disclaim responsibility for bad decisions while proclaiming himself the author of successful ones. He never tried to hide it. He said, "Do as you wish. If things go right, I get the medals; if not, then it's your fault." He spoke the truth. This is what he feels, and he acts accordingly. But a president's work depends on making decisions and all that goes with it, which means assuming the responsibility for the consequences.

Krzysztof Wyszkowski: Wałęsa is personally too weak to be a dictator. A dictator is a person who can accumulate power and use it to rule competently and thoughtfully. Wałęsa is not able to work out a plan for a dictatorship. Not only is he incapable, but he is too lazy. But a dictatorship by proxy is possible. Wałęsa would have to find someone over whom he had complete control, for example, a submissive prime minister with a first-rate economic staff. Then the slogans would be simple.

I have lost my belief in Wałęsa to such a degree that I give credence to the idea that he is trying to solidify his influence in the armed forces, so that he could have its support if needed. He is supporting the old generals, Communists, and the OPZZ and is the last proponent of the old ways on the political scene.

Jarosław Kaczyński: Wałęsa could be dangerous to the nation, and proof of this are his latest statements about the necessity of suspending democracy. In my opinion his group has a destructive effect on our nation. Wałęsa would like to have wide-ranging powers, and it may be that he will be in power for a long time, but there will be limits on it. I think that he would like to take Piłsudski's position: being able to decide about everything but still stand a little to the side.

A referendum could be called, but I don't think this is the time for it. I don't know if he is fully cognizant how the people have tired of him. Yet the results are relative because even though Wałęsa gets low marks, the Sejm does even worse. But in a confrontation between the Sejm and the president, the president would lose and the Sejm would triumph.

How long will he maintain the presidency? At the time I took the position as chief of staff in his office, I told him that he was a temporary president. The new constitution is not in place yet, and it may contain some regulatory provisions. It may say that at the time of its ratification the current president's term of office ends, it may suspend the president's powers for a period of time, or it may give him immediate authority. I will suspend my predictions until the new constitution is in place.

Notes

Translator's Note

1. Maciej Pawlicki, "Poles Apart," *Philadelphia Inquirer Magazine*, March 4, 1990.

2. *Time*, April 8, 1991, and *Newsweek*, March 18, 1991 (international English-language editions). The book was published under the Polish title *Wódz*, which can be variously translated as "the boss," "the leader," or "the chief."

Translator's Introduction

1. John Hackett, *The Third World War: August 1985* (New York: Macmillan 1979).

2. Michael T. Kaufman, "The Importance of General Jaruzelski," *New York Times Magazine*, December 9, 1984.

3. Ursula Obst, "Inside Poland," *Philadelphia Daily News*, February 8–10, 1982.

4. "Interview with Andrzej Gwiazda," *Skorpion* (a Gdańsk underground publication), December 1982–January 1983.

5. P. J. O'Rourke, *Holidays in Hell* (New York: Atlantic Monthly Press, 1988), p. 74.

Introduction

1. The "year of Mazowiecki" lasted approximately from August 24, 1989, to November 25, 1990.

2. The battle against what some termed the monopoly of Solidarity was the axis for political conflict during 1990, an election year. Wałęsa thought that onetime Solidarity people would use the Citizens' Committee movement to create a strong political party that would then monopolize all political activity. Wałęsa was afraid of single-party rule by people who were the old opposition organized into a party based in the Solidarity organization. This issue was oversold and used mainly to advance Wałęsa in the election campaign.

3. Jarosław Kurski was given the job of press spokesman when his predecessor, Piotr Nowina-Konopka, was appointed as a liaison between Solidarity and the government headed by President Jaruzelski. (The position carried the rank of secretary of state.) Kurski had established credentials in the Gdańsk journalistic community, his family was known to Walesa, and he was recommended by Solidarity activists Adam Michnik and Bogdan Borusewicz.

Chapter 1

1. Belweder Palace is a neoclassical building located near Warsaw's Łazienki Park. Since 1918 it has housed government offices of the Polish republic. It currently serves as the office of the Polish president and has some living accommodations. It is roughly analogous to the U.S. White House.

2. *Polityka* started as a publication sanctioned by the Communist party. However, it had a broad liberal outlook permitting, within limits, a diverse range of views to be aired. For the most part its outlook was pragmatic. It slowly evolved from a party publication into one with a social democratic, left-oriented outlook and continued after the PZPR had ceased to exist.

3. The Polish parliament consists of two chambers, the Sejm and the senate (Senat). The senate is the newer of the two, added as a result of the Round Table agreements of 1988. The Sejm consists of 460 deputies, the senate of 100 senators. The Sejm contains seventeen political caucuses. The largest of these is controlled by the Democratic Union party (post-Solidarity democrats) and the Alliance of the Democratic Left (ex-Communists).

4. The First National Solidarity Congress opened on October 8, 1981. On its agenda were plans for the future, practical action, and a plan for reaching a compromise with the government to make Solidarity fit into the Polish scene without being subordinated by the Communist party. Walesa was elected as president of a labor union with 10 million members.

The Second National Solidarity Congress, held in April 1990, was mainly symbolic, a celebration of the union's rebirth. The one substantive issue involved a vote regarding Solidarity's status: It was to remain a labor union and not evolve into a political party. Walesa was once again elected as president of the labor union, which now had only 2 million members.

5. The Catholic church has always had a stabilizing role in the political life of Poland (especially among the opposition groups). Solidarity could not have succeeded without its backing. The bishops played a supporting but crucial role in keeping the various factions talking. The opposition groups pulled together until the Communists were out, then started working on their own agendas.

6. The Citizens' Parliamentary Caucus is an organization of Solidarity-allied Sejm deputies and senators elected during the June 4, 1989, elections. This organization was to be a core of opposition to the Communists. When Mazowiecki became the prime minister, the caucus supported his government. When new parties such as the Center Alliance started to form, the caucus fragmented. The first caucus leader was Bronisław Geremek, who was replaced by Mieczysław Gill when the Democratic Union (Mazowiecki's) party came into being.

7. In 1990 the Solidarity labor union had organized itself by regions and by branches. Each enterprise or factory had its own Solidarity unit, and the units were grouped into geographic regions which were represented on the Solidarity National Commission. Each unit also belonged to an industrial branch (mining, for example) and each branch had its own national commission.

8. The term *liberal* is associated with the pro-change forces in the Polish political scene. Politicians under this label are for reform, a market economy, privatization of industry, and less government interference.

9. The CRZZ (Central Council of Labor Unions) was created by the Communists as an umbrella organization for all the officially recognized labor unions. Because it did not represent the interests of the workers, it was discredited and subsequently dissolved in 1980.

10. The civil militia (the equivalent of the ordinary police) entered a session of the city council in Bydgoszcz and brutally beat council members and others. Among those present were several Solidarity activists, including Jan Rulewski, the chairman of Solidarity for the Bydgoszcz area. The incident caused a drawn-out crisis in relations between Solidarity and the Communist government. Throughout Polish industry, workers announced their readiness to strike. Poland seemed to be edging toward civil war. At the last possible moment, the two sides reached and signed an understanding.

11. KPN (Confederation of Independent Poland), an independent-populist political party founded in 1979, was led by Leszek Moczulski. It is well represented in the Polish parliament.

12. The Round Table was a symbol of government dialogue with the populace. In March 1989, representatives of the Communist government and those of the opposition (mainly Solidarity) negotiated and signed an agreement that set into motion a number of rapid reforms. (These included the relegalization of the Solidarity labor union and a law guaranteeing a plurality of labor unions.) It paved the way for the elections on June 4, 1989, in which the anti-Communist opposition gained ascendancy.

13. *Tygodnik Solidarność* was founded in 1980 as the official press organ of Solidarity. Its first editor was Tadeusz Mazowiecki. On December 13, 1981, with the declaration of martial law, publication was stopped. Reactivated in 1989, again with Mazowiecki as editor, it became the labor union paper. First Jarosław Kaczyński, then Andrzej Goldberg, took over as editor after Mazowiecki became prime minister.

Chapter 2

1. The *left leg* is a phrase Wałęsa often used in reference to the political Left. Wałęsa stressed that a left and right leg are necessary for political life to be stable.

2. *Gazeta Wyborcza* was founded as a publication to promote Solidarity and allied candidates in the 1989 elections. Under Adam Michnik, it grew to become Poland's most widely read newspaper

3. After the coup of 1926, Piłsudski became the overseer of the Polish political scene. He was the final authority among the contending factions and guaranteed a measure of political peace.

4. *Głos Wielkopolski* is a daily newspaper published in Poznań.

5. Rather than birthdays, Poles celebrate name days, many of which fall on the feast days of various saints. Such occasions are often used for family reunions and reconciliations among feuding friends. Over the years, the name day calendar has been secularized, and old Slavic names, such as Lech, have been added.

6. During the parliamentary elections of 1989, local election committees played a vital role in promoting Solidarity candidates for office. After the election these

became citizens' committees united under the Warsaw Citizens' Committee, which is composed of the Solidarity elite. A conference entitled "Etos Solidarności" (Ethos of Solidarity) was convened. Jarosław Kaczyński wrecked the conference by accusing the committee leadership (Wujec, Michnik, and Geremek) of trying to use the citizens' committee movement to create their own political party.

7. The Solidarity Foundation collects funds and conducts activities to foster economic development on behalf of the labor union.

Chapter 3

1. *Po Prostu* was a highly readable student weekly that first appeared during 1956–1958. It was closed down by the Communist government because of its high degree of independence. It was resurrected in 1989 but failed for economic reasons.

2. The administration of Edward Gierek (1970–1980) tried to portray itself as a progressive, modern, socialist regime. This was especially important because the government had embarked on a program of industrial modernization financed by loans from the West. While living conditions in Poland seemed to be improving and consumer products were more plentiful, censorship was increasing, citizens' rights were being curtailed, and political opponents of the regime were being suppressed. The security apparatus was being built up, and corruption flourished within the Communist party.

3. Marie Skłodowska-Curie (1867–1934), the Polish-born physicist who discovered radium and became a two-time Nobel Prize winner; Prince Józef Poniatowski (1763–1813), a Polish national hero who led the Polish troops allied with Napoleon and received the rank of marshal during the battle of Leipzig.

4. Genscher was the German foreign minister until his resignation in 1992. Teltschik was an advisor to Chancellor Helmut Kohl on matters relating to German-Polish relations.

Chapter 4

1. Anna Kurski, a lawyer, was a member of the Solidarity administrative board for the Gdańsk region during 1980–1981. A member of Andrzej Gwiazda's faction in Solidarity, she often criticized Wałęsa when he violated the rules of a democratic organization.

2. Marshal Józef Piłsudski lived in a house in Sulejówek, near Warsaw, from 1922 until he headed the coup in May 1926. Sulejówek has become a symbol for a voluntary withdrawal from political life.

3. The boundaries between political factions are often difficult to pin down, but this is an approximate assessment of the political alignment in Poland. The Left (socialist-oriented) are the post-Communist parties such as the Alliance of the Democratic Left and the Union of Labor. The Polish Peasant party (PSL) is moderate but left-oriented. At the Center are the moderate reformers, such as: the Center Alliance (Jarosław Kaczyński), the Democratic Union party (Mazowiecki), and the Liberal Democratic Congress party. On the Right are parties that have a

nationalistic orientation and advocate far-reaching reform. Among them: the Polish Convention party, the National Christian Union, and the extreme reformist Union of Real Politics.

4. Węsiory is a vacation area in the Kashubian lake district near Gdańsk where Wałęsa owns a summer home.

5. Cyrus Vance was in Poland on behalf the Agency for International Development, to get a firsthand idea of the situation in Poland.

6. *Kultura*, a literary magazine in the Polish language, is published monthly in Paris by Jerzy Gedroyc.

Chapter 5

1. "Dziekania" (literally Deaconry) was a conservative, right-oriented political organization, now dissolved, led by Stanisław Stomma. It had the support of the Catholic church from the mid-1980s until the Round Table negotiations. Its members joined either the Democratic Union party or the Conservative party.

2. *Głos* was the official publication of the Workers' Defense Committee and was published in the period between June 1976 and August 1980.

3. In December 1970 a series of strikes over price increases in Gdańsk (including the shipyards) was put down by force; reportedly, over fifty people were killed by the militia in random shooting incidents.

4. At that time, the ZSL (United Peasant party) had not yet mutated into the PSL (Polish Peasant party). On November 26, 1989, the party called a special congress to accomplish this change.

5. "Family-Cortege-Court" is the tile of an article written by Piotr Wierzbicki, once an avid follower of Wałęsa, who became his foremost critic. The phrase characterizes the Polish political scene in 1990. The *family* were the people from the old KOR, followers of Geremek. The *cortege* were Solidarity activists not linked to KOR. The *court* were those who clustered around Wałęsa.

6. Under the Communist regime, the government was an extension of the Politburo. The Solidarity leadership did not want to replicate this scheme by having Solidarity fill the power vacuum left by the dissolution of the PZPR.

7. The Center Alliance is a political party founded by Jarosław Kaczyński with Wałęsa's tacit approval. ROAD (Citizens' Movement for Democratic Action), a left-oriented party, came to oppose the alliance. ROAD later merged with the Democratic Union party, forming its left wing.

8. At Katyń, Ostaszków, and Starobielsk, thousands of Polish officers, prisoners taken during the Soviet invasion of Poland at the beginning of World War II, were murdered by Soviet security troops in April 1940.

9. Trial of the Sixteen is the name given to a show trial staged in Moscow by Stalin. The principals, sixteen commanders who led the Polish underground during World War II, were lured out by an offer of negotiations and arrested by the Soviet security service.

10. The OPZZ was the government-sanctioned union that replaced Solidarity during the 1980s after martial law was declared. Solidarność '80 is a splinter group

from the original Solidarity union, headed by Marian Jurczyk. Its influence is greatest in northwestern Poland.

11. Miodowicz, the head of the OPZZ, and Jurczyk, the founder of Solidarność 80, went to Słupsk with the hopes of making the most of the political situation.

12. The Organisation de l'Armée Secrète was an underground military organization with an extreme right orientation. In France and Algeria during 1961–1962, it used terrorist acts in an attempt to prevent the withdrawal of French forces from Algeria. It opposed Algerian independence, seeking to maintain French colonial influence.

Chapter 6

1. The Young Poland movement, which harked to a like-named movement from the early 1900s, was popular with students in the 1970s. The Gdańsk organization was absorbed into the Republican Coalition that formed in June 1990. The coalition then became part of Aleksander Hall's Conservative party, which supports a market economy and traditional values.

2. Arłamów is in the Bieszczady Mountains of southeastern Poland. Wałęsa was interned here during 1981–1982.

3. On Polish Radio Wałęsa stated that, if he could, he would lower all prices by 50, even 100 percent. The remark is the summation of the nonsense that Wałęsa is capable of in his public statements.

4. The Triangular Agreement of Poland-Czechoslovakia-Hungary was the subject of an international initiative to bring the three countries closer together. The goal was to improve economic and political cooperation among them and formulate a common policy toward the Western European nations.

5. Solidarność-Chase Bank was founded in July 1990, and is operated by the Polish-American Financial Enterprises Corporation. The majority stockholder is the Solidarity Economic Fund. The other stockholders are Americans, with David T. Chase the largest individual investor. Of Polish extraction, Chase is on the *Forbes* list of the wealthiest people in the United States. Jacek Merkel is the president of the bank.

6. The laws that govern elections to the Sejm are among the world's worst. They call for proportional representation, which leads to the creation of many political parties. Zbigniew Brzeziński has said that this gives rein to the worst aspects of democracy: anarchy and discord.

7. Telegraf was formed by Center Alliance activists with the purpose of gathering funds for their organization. Questionable financial dealings brought disrepute and scandal to the corporation.

Appendix:
"A Man of What Substance?"

Lech Bądkowski (1981)

During a relaxation of censorship in Poland in 1977, Andrzej Wajda, the country's foremost film director, was able to show his new film: Man of Marble. *The subject of the film was the process of creating workers' heroes in the People's Republic of Poland during the 1950s. Polish society knew the facts well; the surprising thing is that now, for the first time, they had been put on film.*

In 1981 Wajda produced a sequel, Man of Iron, *which built on the previous story using the formation of the new labor union, Solidarity, as its background. Though fictional, the film had many factual events running through it. Lech Wałęsa appeared, as himself, in a walk-on scene as a witness at a wedding ceremony. After winning the Golden Palm award at Cannes, the film entered history as a document of Solidarity's birth.*

At this time the proclamation of martial law of December 13, 1981, was still in the future. Most Solidarity activists were still flushed with the success of their victory. This is when Lech Bądkowski, a member of Solidarity's inner circle, wrote his essay, borrowing the title from the Wajda films. "A Man of What Substance?" asked some hard questions about Wałęsa. At that time the international media was creating a national hero for the Poles, a hero for whom they yearned; yet few, only those close to him at the moment, really knew his qualifications and potential.

It is unfortunate that Bądkowski, a fighter for Polish independence, was never able to participate in the first postwar democratic elections in Poland; he died in 1984. But his questions, and the accompanying observations, are still valid. These are the kind of questions that citizens of all democratic countries should ask about the candidates whom they are about to elect to public office.

The changes and additions to the PRL (People's Republic of Poland) constitution, conducted under unexplained conditions of haste during 1975–1976, produced outcries and protest in intellectual circles, especially in the artistic community. A number of petitions were written, circulated, and signed; among the most active were the Warsaw groups. Not being able to put my name to one of those, I decided to write my own petition. I handed it to the chairman of the Voivodship Committee of the National Unity Front[1] in Gdańsk on February 4, 1976. I thought that in the existing formal structure this was the best political address. I sent copies to the press and to groups of people who held important positions in public life. I also distributed copies among my friends.

I received no answer. But'news of my petition somehow spread locally and reached the student community. Then on one spring day last year, two young people came to see me. One was Bogdan Borusewicz, about whom I had already heard.

Then I became more closely interested in the local community of people who had their own views about the reality that surrounded us. The community was small and consisted of people who were not known outside their own limited circle. In addition the main, nearly exclusive role was played by young people.

In 1976 came the increase in prices of food and other consumables, and it raised immediate protests from the workers. The protests were especially strong in Radom and Ursus and were followed by police repression and quasi-legal trials (judges presiding over political trials held under an authoritarian regime can only be called mock law). In September the Workers' Defense Committee (KOR) came into being. Soon Borusewicz became one of its members.

On April 29 or 30, 1978, the founding committee for Free Trade Unions on the Coast (WZZW) was created. It was a group that initiated an authentic workers' movement to support the human and civil rights of the working masses. It was an attempt to give substance, among the workers, to the slogans propagated by KOR. Lech Wałęsa found himself among those people, and that is where I first heard his name, then unknown, but I did not meet him personally.

As far as I know, Wałęsa participated in the founding committee of the Free Trade Unions and signed its declarations, but he was on the periphery of the action. He belonged, but he followed his own direction and for the most part was more of an ally than a member. I must add that at the time the only member of the committee that I did know was Borusewicz. I had never even heard of Anna Walentynowicz.[2]

I met with the larger group of young people at the end of 1978 in connection with the recall action against Błażej Wyszkowski, Krzysztof's brother. Both were active in creating the Free Trade Union founding committee and in its work. Then I met members of another independent movement to which I was attracted—the Young Poland movement, a splinter organization that emancipated itself from the Movement for the Defense of Human and Civil Rights—or, rather, from the leadership of Leszek Moczulski. They were all recent graduates or students: Aleksander Hall, Arkadiusz Rybicki, Dariusz Kobzdej, Magda Modzelewska, Leszek Jankowski (members of the Young Poland movement).

Contacts and meetings slowly increased, and there arose a strange situation in which we heard propagandistic assurances about the fantastic and surprising growth that Poland was experiencing, achievement, improvements in the standard of living; meanwhile, in certain spheres of society the independent movements were growing. And still I had no contact with Wałęsa; I did not know him; I heard nothing about him.

In 1980 the elections to the Sejm were held. In response, the Free Trade Unions and the editors of the *Robotnik Wybrzeża* [Worker of the coast] (a mutation of *Robotnik* [Worker], a KOR publication) published a handbill that called for an end to the ritual of passive voting for the one list of candidates and either crossing off the names or not going to the polling places. (I had long thought that the elections were a sham and did not go to "vote.") The handbill was signed by eight people:

Bogdan Borusewicz, Andrzej Bulc, Joanna Duda-Gwiazda, Andrzej Gwiazda, Alina Pieńkowska, Maryla Płońska, Anna Walentynowicz, and Lech Wałęsa.

Then came May 3. The memory of the day honoring the Polish constitution[3] of 1791—the first in Polish and European history—had been relegated to the realm of things to be forgotten. Now it had again been remembered in Gdańsk—and in some ways in all of Poland—thanks to the Young Poland movement. It was again remembered in 1980. When the handbills were distributed, Wałęsa was twice arrested and held under arrest for forty-eight hours, as were a number of other persons. During the rally to honor the Third of May Constitution at the Sobieski[4] Monument, two persons gave speeches: Dariusz Kobzdej and Tadeusz Szczudłowski. Both were sentenced to three months in prison. The matter was appealed to the regional court in Gdańsk, but the sentence was allowed to stand.

While Kobzdej and Szczudłowski were in jail, they went on a hunger strike and were force-fed. Meanwhile, at the Church of the Virgin Mary, prayer vigils were held for them. Lech Wałęsa was one of the participants. It was on a July night after one such prayer service, when the participants were standing outside the church, that Aleksander Hall pointed out Wałęsa to me. He did this because I was interested, not to make his acquaintance.

My resulting impression was that Wałęsa was not a person who was numbered among the top level of leaders in the organization. I had heard that he was actively involved and exceptional for his aggressive approach in the still small group of worker activists in the Free Trade Unions, but not as a leading personality. I believe that at the time no one thought him to have leadership potential, because I received no prompting to take a closer look at him. I must, however, add that at that time I was almost exclusively interested in the theoretical and ideological problems of the democracy movement in Poland, and in its chances of influencing certain institutions in the government to restrain them from repressive acts. In this respect I was very lightly involved in organizational work except for distributing uncensored publications and participating in private meetings. That is why my knowledge about the activities of the founding committee of the Free Trade Unions was incomplete, and the only people I knew from that group were Borusewicz and Krzysztof Wyszkowski.

(At this time I must add the following: it is not an easy task to formulate a list of the founding members, and it is subject to interpretation because in this case, just as in similar situations, the amount of involvement varied from member to member, and the appropriate papers documenting the founding were never filed in the appropriate office. In addition, even among the founders there often will be disagreements, and people resign or are thrown out. I was, for example, told that Krzysztof Wyszkowski was removed. I have also encountered the belief that Wałęsa was not numbered among the original founders of the committee. And in addition, it is well known that failure is an orphan, whereas success has many jealous fathers. After all is said and done, there will be those who will gladly take credit without having made a contribution, while denying it to those who actually worked. A separate problem deserving some scrutiny is that during the formation of the committee and later of the Solidarity labor union, as in any spontaneous activity, there were many people with troublemaking tendencies who were opposed to the current order. I had mentioned this problem, in reference to our realities, several times on other occasions.)

At the beginning of July 1980, the introduction of badly concealed price increases (so-called commercial prices) for food products brought a time of turbulence throughout Polish society. Strikes broke out in many cities and ended only when wages were raised in enterprises that had been struck. Finally, on August 14 a sit-down strike took place at the Gdańsk shipyard (also known as the Lenin Shipyard), and this precipitated analogous strikes at other enterprises resulting in a general strike in the Tri-City [Gdańsk-Gdynia-Sopot] area that quickly spread along the Baltic Coast. (The spontaneously formed workers' self-governments managed to exclude from the strike those services vital to a normal life. This included rail transport, health services, and power.)

At the beginning of the shipyard strike, I heard about Wałęsa, but in general terms because as a currently unemployed worker from the Gdańsk shipyard, he had found himself inside the shipyard among the most active strike organizers on August 14. On the following day he headed up the strike committee, quickly taking a leading role that continued to grow, encompassing a greater sphere. The shortage of information was due to a campaign of disinformation conducted by the media at that time. In the television news there was a short item about a "work stoppage" at the Gdańsk shipyard but nothing more. In my daily journal from August 15 I wrote: "As far as I understand, Lech Wałęsa has moved to head the strike committee. Anna Walentynowicz is active as well." Something was happening.

Stanisław Załuski and I found our way into the Gdańsk shipyard for the first time on August 17, late in the afternoon. It was Sunday, a decisive day, as it turned out, for the continuation of the strike. And then I still did not get to speak to Wałęsa, who was sleeping, trying to get some rest after a very strenuous time. But I did get to meet Anna Walentynowicz.

From the conversations I had there, it turned out that Wałęsa had without a doubt taken a leading position.

On August 21, after preparations that took several days, there was a meeting of Gdańsk writers (at least of those who were notified and managed to come). A proposal for a proclamation was discussed and the final wording decided on around 3:00 p.m. A large group of signers, members of the Polish Writers' Union and the Youth Club, went to the shipyard. Our first stop was the BHP [Health and Safety] hall, so called because this is where instruction in work safety and hygiene was given. This is where the general assembly of the Interenterprise Strike Committee (MKS) was based. At the gate we had to identify ourselves and explain the purpose of our visit, and by the time we reached the hall our presence was already announced. Wałęsa, standing at the podium microphone surrounded by the presidium members, announced to the delegates that writers had come to say something important and invited us up on the platform. He added something else, saying only to me something like: "Well, finally, our literati are here." After I read our proclamation, which was greeted with enthusiasm, Wałęsa embraced me most sincerely.

This is how I finally came face to face with the leader who in the next few days was to become one of the best-known Poles in his own country and around the world.

I have written about the time before August 21, 1980, to bring out two things. One is the difficulties and the slowness of the process involved in meeting people who were active in various social movements. First, this was due to unfavorable conditions where the means for communicating views were unavailable and the social structures themselves were artificial and badly formed. Second, Lech Wałęsa was only in the process of becoming a leader of the workers' social movement during August and September 1980. Before that he was still a person totally unknown to society at large and anyone outside the small group of worker colleagues in the workplace and activists in the founding committee of the Free Trade Unions on the Coast.

Today I know a lot more about the activists of the Free Trade Unions from before August 21, 1980, but this I have learned from documents and later conversations. But here I have presented the level of my knowledge, especially about Wałęsa, as it was then.

Awareness of the two things described above illustrates one of the great problems faced by a Poland in the process of internal reform. During the thirty-six years since the end of World War II, after the long period of building up the third Polish republic, we were forced to give extremely important positions of social trust to people about whom we knew very little, because we had no time to learn about them and they had no way to show us that they were worthy of our trust. This refers not only to Wałęsa but to all the activists in Solidarity and all the other organizations that started to wake up as if they had been in a prolonged sleep. A strike, or any act of defiance, can attest to a person's character, but it is a one-sided test that says nothing about the person's intelligence or ability to act constructively or about the individuals who are involved in a strike. The same can be said about those persons who rose to prominence during the tidal wave of the August events.

This situation, superficially absurd after thirty-six years of the existence of a nation and a regime, also applies to the Communist party, because its leaders, on various levels, suddenly found themselves on the way out while their replacements were not able to tell the people anything through their names alone. This was a manifestation of the absence of democracy in public life.

Now I would like to describe just what kind of man and leader I found Wałęsa to be, after I had nine months to associate with and observe him closely.

First of all he talks a lot, and gives interviews eagerly, perhaps too eagerly. This observation is first because the quantity of his public pronouncements, at least those that I know—and I am sure I don't know them all—creates the impression of extreme gabbiness but could also lead to erroneous conclusions. It seems to me that he is neither as open or as easily understood as he would like people to think he is. This attitude may be understood in several ways. Whether the "number one" person in the labor movement wants to or not, he must be a political person in a nation with such a system and such a delicate situation as Poland's. Wałęsa's inclination to talk at length can be, in a few words, an offensive shield he uses to hide the deficiencies in his leadership. The striking thing is his readiness to repeat phrases instantly in negotiations and discussions. Often these phrases are good, to the point, sometimes even inspired, but often they are evasions that hide the lack of an answer or even the lack of knowledge about a subject. Wałęsa does not like to reveal that he does not know something, that he has to think about something, that he would like to confer with someone first.

With this trait there is a corresponding mobility. He walks quickly, gestures in a lively fashion, and talks fast. He likes to joke around; he likes humor; even when aimed at himself, but this does not indicate that he is able to accept criticism. In personal relations he tries to be courteous, even though brusqueness is part of his character. He seems not to have got the message yet on the subject of personal relations. He does not listen with sufficient care to the things that are said to him, especially if they do not concur with his own opinions. With all this, he is, and it may seem contradictory, self-assured and even conceited.

The seeds of combativeness must have been in him always, otherwise he would not have found himself in the Free Trade Union movement and then moved to the head of the Gdańsk shipyard strike. After all, he had not worked there for the last few years. His advancement, no doubt, was speeded along by a favorable turn of events, especially his election as the chairman of the Interenterprise Strike Committee, which included the workplaces in the Gdańsk coastal area and a number of enterprises distributed around Poland. The striking workers and all of those taking part in the protest wanted unity and sought leadership. All eyes turned toward Gdańsk, especially to the Gdańsk shipyard, because this is where the events of December 1970 took place. This is where the protest started. The strike of 1970 was brutally suppressed with bloody results, but it was effective. The expectation that "something would happen in Gdańsk" was based on the principle that once, in the past, a significant event did take place there. It was irrational but universal. A favorable situation arose, and Wałęsa walked into it. Whether he was aware of the far-reaching consequences of this turn of events is another matter—who at that time could have correctly predicted the way things would fall? But it is a fact that he went in and won.

At the beginning, no one thought much about a long-term program for the movement, which grew out of a protest staged by the working masses. The list of twenty-one demands, hastily drawn up, was enough. All that came about later from a new and quickly evolving situation was due to improvisation that succeeded with extraordinary luck. Such an unplanned and extremely favorable factor was the self-offered assistance of the intellectual community. (To Wałęsa's credit he instantly realized the value of such aid and accepted it.) And Wałęsa took the leadership position without wavering, without having any organizational support for such a great undertaking. Still, I believe he did not understand the size of this undertaking and its possible effects. In this case his combativeness served him well, though it led to his taking great risks, risks that would have made the flesh crawl for a more sedate person.

One must add to this combativeness the ability to think like a leader. Wałęsa has it in his blood, in a people's version. He can stand before a crowd and speak quite freely, as if he were talking to several close friends. This put him into the position of a "people's tribune." I was the witness of several of his speeches; I stood right beside him. The listeners reacted in a lively fashion, with enthusiasm.

But to tell the truth there was nothing in his words that would rouse the people, reveal something new, or inspire them to action. I listened and observed without being affected because these speeches contained slogans and phrases already well known and used turns of speech designed for wide acceptance—sometimes in the style of stage actors—and the listeners swallowed every word and gesture and replied with joy, emotion, delight. It was surely because he spoke simply, in their language, as any one of them would speak, but just a little better. It worked because over the years they had heard too much dead and swollen language and now were finally hearing common, everyday human speech containing its share of linguistic errors. For them it was unusual and revealing because it was not a bureaucrat but their leader speaking, one from their own ranks and of their own choosing.

This was not the only thing that brought him great success. Other activists spoke this way, too, and were listened to willingly and applauded. Wałęsa has a gift, often called charisma. All will confirm this. It is hard to describe this inborn gift of God which is priceless. Such a gift has long been recognized and has become the subject of sociological study—and in earlier times of religious studies. Few individuals have it, and its range of effectiveness varies. In this regard Wałęsa holds the Polish record since the time of Piłsudski[5] or … Gomułka.[6] Today, few remember the popularity that Gomułka enjoyed in October 1956, how charismatic a person he seemed. His magic disappeared very quickly.

Charisma cannot be bought, but carefully or instinctively it can be strengthened, and its range can be extended. Wałęsa did this very thing by ostentatiously showing his religious faith. It rendered an excellent effect as a contrast to the official secularism (and semiofficial atheism) of the government that was under siege. The field masses, the singing of religious hymns, holy pictures, praying the rosary all created an atmosphere of heightened spirits in the face of danger.

But I must make an important comment here. Charisma, as understood by sociology, is a dangerous factor. It is based on traits that are valued and supported by society, but those traits in a person recognized as charismatic may be real or faked, or there may be a mixture of both. The objective criteria may only be measured after the fact. It cannot be excluded, then, that Wałęsa's great success in part or as a whole was based and continues to be based on appearances, delusions, and wishful thinking. The question is, How will he line up with the truth?

At the end of April 1981 *Czas* [Time],[7] a weekly, printed an interview between myself and its editor, Tadeusz Bolduan, under the heading "The Hunger for Moral Leadership." This conversation took place in mid-January. Bolduan started with the following statement: "I am convinced that the appropriate leader in these times, in face of the challenges before Solidarity, is not Lech Wałęsa."

I replied:

Lech Wałęsa [as leader] is a historical accident, a case of history playing tricks with us. The dilemma lies in the fact that the hunger for moral leadership in Poland has caused Wałęsa to be elevated to incredible heights, and in this case we cannot try to sober up the populace, because we would be depriving them of the very thing for which they fought so hard, and received with such joy. But at the same time it is apparent that this man, even though he is the symbol of a breakthrough, is not the long-awaited leader. To make the jump from a repressed unemployed worker to a "man of the year" created by the Western media and placed on the covers of illustrated magazines that have circulations in the millions, to give interviews to the largest news agencies in the world, to the weeklies and dailies and not undergo corruption—that would require a man with enormous reserves of inner culture.

Fragments of my reply created a small storm among Solidarity activists, which possibly was also used to provide a cover for the anger caused by the answer to Bolduan's next question: "What about the others?" My answer was: "There are no other people there who are at the right intellectual level. After all there is really nothing strange about it, because where would one find leaders in such an environment?"

I must stress that the thing that escaped notice was that I was speaking about the historical accident. Wałęsa did not prepare himself for his eventual role. He did not seek this position by climbing up one rung at a time, over the years, improving himself, studying, learning the key problems in politics and the politics of the larger sphere. In our recent history Wincenty Witos[8] was a leading self-taught politician, but he came to occupy higher and higher positions in the social and political hierarchy gradually. And he proved himself to a greater part of society. I believe that Wałęsa never imagined that he would take the position that fell to him, although today he has said, and even believed, differently.

This was what chance, fate, history, necessity—or providence, if you prefer—has wrought. I also believe that the "hunger for moral leadership" has given him the role of "the little corporal" in Polish society from the middle of August 1980 to ... who knows? (Just to make sure, "the little corporal" was the appellation given to Napoleon Bonaparte by his worshipers.) I do not want to play with suppositions, but I only want to make the comment that the "incredible elevation" of Wałęsa poses further expectations, expectations that could only be fulfilled by a genius.

I did not yet exhaust all the circumstances that came together at that time. In August 1980 not only Polish eyes were looking toward Gdańsk. The whole world was looking in that direction, remembering December 1970. And there was more: The combination of Gdańsk in 1939 and Gdańsk in 1980, as both a danger and a possibility, was the thing that stimulated world opinion, thanks to the mass media. The strike that enveloped Gdańsk (that is, the Gdańsk shipyard) behaved differently from the strike in Szczecin or the shipyard located there (which was the headquarters of the Interenterprise Workers' Committee). In Szczecin the gates were sealed and the journalists, except for some local ones, were cut off. Gdańsk received a crowd of reporters, first foreign then domestic, and they were immediately welcomed.

The entry of the international media assured that the Gdańsk strike would receive a lot of notoriety, and so would Wałęsa's persona. I do not call this good or bad—it is a fact. Wałęsa became known around the world overnight.

The above words are based in some measure on documents (mainly private documents) and on personal experiences and impressions. I would also like to add that since my first face-to-face meeting with Wałęsa, I had a positive orientation toward him and the best intentions. Personally, I was not looking for moral leadership—this being a complex concept that would not appear until later—or political direction, but I was looking for the power and organizational effectiveness serving a plan of action.

Let's bypass the subject of a plan of action. But I must say that Wałęsa, by my observations, is not organizationally minded and does not even have an understanding of the need for an ordered and productive organization. He is a self-satisfied improviser. A daily calendar and an appointment schedule are totally alien to him. He talks with dozens of people in chance conversations and wastes time on unnecessary events, but he can be several hours late for an important high-level meeting.

In the Interenterprise Founding Committee (MKZ, the successor organization to the MKS), disorder rules. Those with business there know it well. In the beginning it was all excused, because it was understood that at the time it could not be otherwise. But months passed, and the people who went there were still being shuffled around, often because of simple incompetence. More and more of them became disillusioned and went away cursing. Wałęsa pays no attention to his backyard, whose appearance gives testimony to the poor state of things. The problem is to decide whether this is due to a lack of understanding of the need for an efficient functional organization or to Wałęsa's feeling of being above such things and viewing the daily problems as being of little importance. De Gaulle dealt personally only with the most important political questions; he termed all the other things, especially the economy, as "commissariat," which from the lips of a general-president had a tone of disregard, nearly contempt. Wałęsa probably never heard of de Gaulle's aversion to the things he regards as pleasant, but his attitude is similar.

On August 15, 1980, or two weeks after the creation of the Solidarity labor union, I wrote a letter to Wałęsa. I felt that the negotiating position should be expressed in writing and broken down into individual points that could be easily read and considered. This would give better results than discussions without such preparation.

This was the letter:

Dear Chairman and Friend:

We have been working together for a while now, in rushed conditions that have accelerated our getting to know each other. I have decided that it is necessary and important that I should write down a few comments that, if you consider them pertinent, should be shared with members of the presidium and other persons who are acting in concert with us or are supporting us.

1. It is high time to organize the way the presidium functions. Our resources are being expended in a chaotic and wasteful manner. The number of meetings must be cut down and individual meetings limited to a specific period of time. In addition:

a. At the beginning of each meeting the appointed chairman should be introduced, and all must conform to his dictates in a formal sense.

b. A list of discussion topics should be established, leaving a small reserve for other matters during a "free expression" period at the end of the meeting.

   c. Enforce an "iron rule" over the speakers and maintain the order in which
they come up to speak.

   d. Combat the tendency to speak interminably and off the topic.

2. At the presidium meetings only the following may participate:

   a. members of the presidium

   b. experts called by the presidium

   c. guests invited by name

   3. Meetings of the presidium should be recorded. Until we can afford a detailed
record to be made, we should at least start a book documenting work (which would
list the persons and actions for which they have responsibility) and decisions made.

   4. Financial matters need to be organized. A budget should be drawn up, at
least in framework, and money disbursed accordingly. The larger expenditures
should be approved by the presidium separately. Otherwise we may find ourselves
in trouble and run the risk of bad public opinion. I think it would be good to
publicize the provisional budget for the period through December 31, 1980.

   5. In the near future a reorganization of the presidium should be considered, to
allocate responsibilities and streamline the work. I believe that this important step
should wait but that a secretary of the presidium should be selected (from among its
members) and a director for its office who would be responsible for the administrative functions and eventually a manager for its quarters who would care for the fur-
nishing, maintenance, and cleaning. These people must have the highest
qualifications and work on the basis of a contract.

   6. The political position of our MKZ is very difficult, delicate, and pregnant
with consequences. The understanding of August 31, 1980, states that the labor
unions associated under us "do not constitute a political party." But to me it is clear
that even though they will not be a political party, they will be a factor—an
important factor—in the social and political life of our country. And then there is the
fact that our situation is a combination of internal Polish politics and those of the
international arena. It has sharply manifested itself during the strike. It is manifest-
ing itself now and will continue to do so in the future. A good measure of this is the
intensity of the interest exhibited by the foreign press.

   I believe that one should not ask (especially only three days after the signing of
the understanding and without discussing the matter first) Mr. Jacek Kuroń to
become an expert advisor to the MKZ presidium. He is a person, doubtlessly very
worthy, but controversial and oriented in an exclusively political direction. It is
good that things have turned out in a way where Mr. Kuroń's invitation to be an
advisor has expired.

   All the political problems that we will face—I am sure they will not diminish—
will require careful consideration before a group decision is made.

   7. The eyes of all Poland are turned to the MKZ in Gdańsk. This is where people
expect inspiration, counsel, example, and support. A symbolic and moving example
of this feeling is the registration of an Independent Union of National Museum
Workers of Warsaw with the Gdańsk MKZ.

   This situation, which we did not foresee and for which we were not prepared,
has placed an enormous responsibility on us. We will either measure up to the
situation and the responsibility with honor, or we will find ourselves on the pages
of history as a group of noble amateurs who could not come to terms with their own
significance and lost, closing this beautiful period whose significance was much
reduced. One way or another, history will not pass us by in silence.

   The awareness of the above alternative must always be with us and steer all our
actions.

My sincere regards.

The points about organizational and financial matters are self-evident. It may seem strange to some that I had to enumerate such obvious things. But they illustrate the resulting situation. Improvements were made at a slow rate and only in a limited area, mostly through the initiatives of Wałęsa's associates on the presidium. But when he read my letter (he did it at a meeting at which I was present, so I know), he put it in his pocket and did not react. Later, on several occasions, I tried without success to talk to him about things in general. On the other hand he did not wish to accept my resignation as a member of the presidium. I thought that this might have been an attempt on his part to hold in reserve a person who might yet be useful for his own political purposes.

Wałęsa's actions are extremely difficult to predict, and this example illustrates what it is like to support him. For some reason—which I did not try to find out—the supporters of Jacek Kuroń tried to take over the presidium of the Gdańsk MKZ, acting to oust Wałęsa or at least to force him to become a tool for their own political purposes. At the October 25, 1980, meeting of the presidium, five workers from the Gdańsk shipyard, Solidarity members, were introduced and a demand was issued to give them voting rights. This was tantamount to making them members of the presidium. This was against the rules; only the general assembly of MKZ delegates could approve such a mandate, but the disorder in the organization favored the move. Wałęsa took a strong stand against this move and argued correctly that he, too, could bring in five people of his own choice and give them voting rights. When during the hot discussion I took Wałęsa's side and used the words *coup d'état*, Bogdan Borusewicz, the leader of the Gdańsk Kuroń faction (brought into the presidium by Wałęsa just recently) was outraged, but it was clear that he did not have anything intelligent to say even though he and his faction stuck with their absurd proposal.

Finally, Wałęsa, seeing that the majority of those present would support the motion or at least abstain from voting and induct the workers—and this was quite likely in view that those present were not well informed in democratic principles for organizations—said that he was terminating the meeting and leaving and that those who were "with him" should join him in walking out. Of the twenty persons present, only three went with him: Ewa Górska, Wojciech Gruszecki, and I. Later a fourth joined us, but he was shaky and would have liked to be on both sides. A short time later he left the presidium altogether.

The die was cast. At least it seemed so. We went to Wałęsa's room to have a conference. I expressed the view that we must take this turn of events to the MKZ Gdańsk general assembly and persuade them to dismiss the plenum and elect a new one. Wałęsa said that this is what he decided. I asked him if he had thought about suitable candidates for the new plenum; he said he had the names.

Then we prepared a program for the meeting of the National Commission of Understanding,[9] which was to meet in Gdańsk on October 27. It was an urgent assignment because these events were taking place during the attempt to register the Solidarity labor union in spite of government opposition. Then what to do with the situation in the Gdańsk presidium? When to call the MKZ general assembly to make the changes? Wałęsa decided that, as a test, a second meeting of the presidium should be called on the very same day. He asked me to inform the members.

At 6:00 p.m. the second meeting was convened. From the first to the last moment of the meeting, it seemed that the events of the early afternoon never took place. No one made a comment about the bitter dispute—or how to resolve it. Among adults this was unusual behavior. The three who at the critical moment went to his aid received no explanation from Wałęsa, and he probably never even thought that he had a moral duty to supply one. Much later, when I brought this incident to his attention, reminding him that such behavior tends to alienate loyal and supportive people, he explained in his typically animated and unclear way that between the first and second meeting "they" came to him and "begged him on their knees" to forget about the incident.

I speculated that Wałęsa usually was not sure of having his way, or he may not have had enough trusted candidates for the new presidium, and finally he did not understand the necessity for creating order at the directorate level where members should not behave like conspirators or children. The examples of Wałęsa's inconsistency, carelessness, and lack of preparation are many. But I am not writing a history of early Solidarity; I only cite a few events that illustrate the person from a little-known angle. The question is whether and how much he has learned since that time.

In my opinion Lech Wałęsa has many serious flaws and shortcomings. Perhaps he could start working on himself if he were aware of them, but first he would have to acknowledge that these flaws exist. This would not be easy because he thinks highly of himself, likes to brag, and claims credit for all successes (including the dousing of the Karlino oil-field fire)[10] while leaving the failures to others. He is jealous of his position as number one and shows it at every occasion, which irritates the other activists. He will compromise and make concessions only with the church. This is a separate problem, a very complicated and delicate one, which I will not explore at this time. All I can say is that the church often had a positive influence, but excessive deference and piety led to criticism not only from those in the group who were clear-headed, but from his churchgoing associates (who were in the majority) as well.

Speaking in general terms, I see him as a man of instinct, not of intellect. To be sure, in my opinion, he is a man of considerable intelligence, but he has never devoted himself to improving and developing it. In the past the circumstances were not favorable. Today, there is insufficient time and desire, and he surely does not recognize the need. In addition, he is unable to manage his time in a way that would allow him to spend some time on himself. And then there is his position as the "people's tribune," who knows all, can do all, and must be accepted without criticism. That is why instinct, in which he is no doubt richly endowed, outstrips his intellect.

Thanks to this instinct he can compose the incredible replies that appear in his speeches and that I mentioned already. Thanks to this instinct he could repeatedly make hard decisions and impose his will on those opposing him as well as those supporting him. An extremely poignant example was the defusing of a potentially dangerous social and political conflict that waited in the wings after the events of March 19, 1981, in Bydgoszcz. A general strike encompassing the entire country (called for March 31) was imminent after a warning strike took place on March 27. An agreement reached between Wałęsa and Mieczysław Rakowski on March 30 prevented a dangerous event at the last moment. Wałęsa showed at that time that he could take responsibility. He took a great risk in exceeding his authority, but he took the responsibility and was later criticized by the National Commission of Understanding.

Perhaps he should be called a fighter—to whom reflexes, quick and sure movement, and the desire to shine with success are important. I could summarize this further: He is a man who fights at the crucial moment, at the very peak, when things are most exciting and bright. He is much weaker when it comes to daily toil, the maneuvering for position, which requires continual effort, intelligent and precise organization, but where there are no shining moments.

In the first half of May 1981, at one of the meetings, I talked about Solidarity's problems and about Wałęsa, not leaving out some of the errors or omissions. And I was accused of fomenting "Polish hell." (The joke with which this expression is linked is universal and there is no need to repeat it.)[11]

I believe that this national caricature (of being pulled down just when one manages to rise a little) is much overdone. Similar flaws are common in other societies as well. And that which is an asset in one situation may be a liability in another, and the reverse. But if we compare ourselves with the Germans, Russians, British, French, and so on, we must remember the unfavorable circumstances under which we had to exist as a nation during the last few hundred years, especially the difficult experiences of our recent past. These have contributed greatly to many pathological phenomena, one rather unimportant fragment of which is the so-called Polish hell. The application of this term to "Wałęsa's circumstances" testified to the amount of gossip that was circulating about him. Some of this gossip created a most unflattering, or even demonic, picture of Wałęsa; my critical comments were categorized as belonging to the same class.

I never bothered with gossip. I wrote about facts, interpreting them according to my best—though subjective—judgment. Wałęsa is a new arrival on the public scene, and he came in quickly in a leading role on a national scale, without any preparation. He who wishes to ignore the necessity for preparation may do so. He who wishes to believe in miracles may do so—this will be a manifestation of pure voluntarism, if I may use the word that has been so popular here in the past year. Outside of the learned men, no one understands it, but since it refers without exception to the old regime, everyone has attached the wrong meaning to it, a meaning equal to "self-will," "lawlessness," and "despotism." Often it fits. Abandoning the semantic digression, it must be noted that voluntarism is a much deeper and more complicated concept. Generally speaking, in social science it refers to the conviction about the rule of human will over the laws of nature and society, the absolute rule of the subjective factor. This is an easy entry into the cult of the individual, something we are already familiar with.

Wałęsa, without a doubt, is an individual, and he creates the appearance of a powerful person. The fact that he creates this impression is not proof that he is a strong person. Before him are many dangers; not all can be overcome with instinct or talking circles around opponents or a strong will. Wałęsa's enthusiastic supporters should remember that by elevating him to a national pedestal where no criticism can reach him and bestowing him with their unwavering faith, expecting a miracle, they have cut off his legs. They have taken from him only the things that fit their own image of him. Wałęsa said that "we will show them another Japan." In truth he never kept this outlandish promise, but neither did he clarify, explain, or update the phrase. Very well, we will show them. Let his worshipers work as hard, live as frugally, and be as disciplined as the Japanese— for years. Who really believes it, and who is going to make it come true? He said it; it was effective and without meaning, because you can't have Japan without the Japanese.

Taking all that I have said here under consideration and adding to it the incredibly complicated conditions of the Polish reality today, one can put it on the scales and observe how they rise and fall. From this I came out with the view that among all the leading persons in the Solidarity trade union Lech Wałęsa is the most outstanding and, in a drastic contraction, the best. In the most critical moments he showed a feeling of responsibility for the nation's fate. Without a doubt he was reminded of this responsibility from within—this was due to Cardinal Wyszyński, Poland's primate—but in the end he had to understand this and take it up.

The Wałęsa phenomenon will be studied in great depth and from all possible sides in the foreseeable future.

But in the end the most important thing is Solidarity, the great social movement that in Poland has reached down to the nation's roots and into all realms of life. The power and effectiveness of this movement depend on all of us taken together, on society as a whole, on our ability to put it into practice, on our strength to maintain the opposition—not on any individual, no matter how brilliant. This most important matter is an undertaking that will continue for years.

Notes

1. The National Unity Front, a Communist-sponsored organization, was supposed to represent Polish society on the political scene. In reality it served as a means of nullifying the opposition.

2. Anna Walentynowicz was a crane operator and labor activist involved in the Free Labor Unions. Her firing sparked the events of August 1980 at the Gdańsk shipyard.

3. The Third of May Constitution of 1791 was a progressive document inspired in part by the U.S. Constitution and the American experience. Its approval so worried the European powers that it led to the partition of Poland and its eventual disappearance as a nation-state until its reemergence after World War I.

4. Jan III Sobieski (1630–1696) was a Polish king who relieved the siege of Vienna by the Turks and as a consequence eliminated the Ottoman threat to Europe.

5. Józef Piłsudski (1867–1935) was an activist in the cause of Polish independence and later head of the Polish government.

6. Władysław Gomułka (1905–1982) was a Polish Communist activist who was on the scene before World War II and became the head of the Polish postwar Communist government. Deposed for his nationalistic stance by the party in 1948, he returned to power as first

secretary of the PZPR after a series of strikes in Poznań turned violent in 1956. He fell from power again when his government used force against the strikers in Gdańsk in 1970.

7. *Czas*, published during 1987–1981, was an illustrated weekly that dealt with social, cultural, and political issues. It was dissolved with the onset of martial law. Most of its staff later worked for *Tygodnik Gdański* (Gdańsk weekly).

8. Wincenty Witos (1871–1945) was a peasant activist during the interwar period. He led the peasant movement and was the founder of the original prewar PSL (Polish Peasant party).

9. The National Commission of Understanding was the body that steered and coordinated Solidarity activities during 1980–1981.

10. On December 9, 1980, an oil gusher at the Karlino drilling site (located between Szczecin and Koszalin) ignited and burned for over a week, despite various attempts to extinguish it.

11. A certain political joke made the rounds in 1980: Why are there no guards in Polish hell? Because the Poles themselves will pull down anyone who would try to get out of the pit. They can't stand social climbers.

The expression *Polish hell* has come to mean a situation in which no one is permitted to rise above his station even though this might mean an improvement in the common condition.

Suggested Readings

Ascherson, Neal. *The Polish August: The Self-Limiting Revolution*. New York: Viking Press, 1981.

Craig, Mary. *Lech Wałęsa and His Poland*. New York: Continuum, 1987.

Goodwyn, Lawrence. *Breaking the Barrier: The Rise of Solidarity in Poland*. New York: Oxford University Press, 1991.

Gwertzman, Bernard, and Michael T. Kaufman. *The Collapse of Communism*. New York: Times Books–Random House, 1989.

Kaufman, Michael T. *Mad Dreams, Saving Graces*. New York: Random House, 1989.

Steven, Stewart. *The Poles*. New York: Macmillan, 1982.

Tischner, Józef. *The Spirit of Solidarity*. San Francisco: Harper and Row, 1984.

Wałęsa, Lech. *A Way of Hope*. New York: Henry Holt, 1987.

——————— . *The Struggle and the Triumph*. New York: Arcade, 1992.

Weschler, Lawrence. *Passion of Poland: From Solidarity to the State of War*. Pantheon Books, New York, 1984.

Glossary of Names

Jacek Ambroziak — Minister and the chief of the Council of Ministers in the Mazowiecki government.

Lech Bądkowski — Journalist, author. A soldier during the defensive campaign of 1939, later a member of the Polish armed forces abroad. Member of the Gdańsk shipyard strike committee in August 1980. Wałęsa's first press spokesman. A moral role model for the opposition groups and underground press activists operating on the Polish Baltic Coast. Died in 1984.

Leszek Balcerowicz — Minister of finance in the governments of Mazowiecki and Bielecki. The creator of an austerity economic program. An outstanding political personage. Recipient of the Pro Memoris medal at a gathering of the European Council in Strasbourg in recognition of his achievements in economics. The author of over fifty scientific works published in Poland and abroad.

Roman Bartoszcze — An activist on behalf of the peasants. In 1990 he became the leader of the Polish Peasant party (PSL).

Ryszard Bender — Professor of modern history at the Catholic University in Lublin. An activist on behalf of Polish and Catholic causes.

Krzysztof Bielecki — Trained as an economist. A Solidarity activist, the leader of the Liberal Democratic Congress party. A member of the Polish-American Industrialization Fund. Prime minister from January to December 1991. Currently serving as a Sejm deputy.

Bogdan Borusewicz — Trained as a historian. A legend in the Gdańsk area for his strong stance in opposing the Communist government. Founder of the Free Labor Unions. Inspired the August 1980 strike that led to the creation of Solidarity. A member of the strike committee in the Gdańsk shipyard. Solidarity activist and later one of the union's underground leaders. Sejm deputy.

Zbigniew Bujak — Worker and Solidarity activist. Leader of the committee that established the Mazowsze branch of Solidarity. A legend of the underground movements. Arrested in May 1986. Later a negotiator of the Round Table agreements. Parliamentary representative from his own, small, left-of-center party.

Andrzej Celiński — An activist in the democratic opposition. An associate of Wałęsa. Senator and member of the Democratic Union party.

Wiesław Chrzanowski — Professor of law at the Catholic University in Lublin. The leader of the Christian National Union party. Marshal of the Sejm.

Franciszek Cybula — Priest and chaplain at the Belweder Palace and Wałęsa's personal confessor. Always present at meetings, he is exceptionally reserved and uncritical toward Wałęsa.

Józef Czyrek — Minister of state for international policy in the Communist government formed by Jaruzelski after the declaration of martial law.

Bronisław Dąbrowski — Archbishop; secretary of the Polish episcopate since 1965. One of the closest associates of Cardinal Stefan Wyszyński and Cardinal Glemp.

Marek Dąbrowski — Sejm deputy; member of the Democratic Union party. The vice-minister of finance in the Mazowiecki government.

Andrzej Drzycimski — Coauthor of Wałęsa's biography, *A Way of Hope*. Interned during martial law. The press spokesman to Wałęsa after Kurski's resignation, he continued in that position after Wałęsa ascended to the presidency.

Jan Dworak — Onetime chief editor of the *Tygodnik Solidarność*, dismissed by Wałęsa.

Marek Edelman — Doctor of medicine who received an honorary degree from Yale University. The last living leader of the Warsaw ghetto uprising. Solidarity activist. A member of the Citizen's Committee. Active in the Democratic Union party.

Lech Falandysz — Professor of criminal law, the chief of the law staff in the president's office.

Tadeusz Fiszbach — Activist of the PZPR, leader of the splinter group that became the Social Democratic Union party.

Władysław Frasyniuk — Driver and auto mechanic. The coorganizer of a strike at one of the bus depots in Wrocław in 1980. Solidarity activist and leader of Lower Silesia Solidarity. Member of the Solidarity National Commission. A legend of the underground movement. Twice arrested during martial law. Vice-chairman of the Democratic Union party. Parliamentary representative.

Bronisław Geremek — Historian, lecturer at the Sorbonne and several U.S. universities. A member of the Polish and French PEN. Expert advisor to the interenterprise strike committee in Gdańsk and one of the leading advisors to Solidarity and Wałęsa. Interned during martial law, later arrested. One of the founding members of the Citizens' Committee and an architect of the Round Table. Leader of the Citizens' Parliamentary Caucus. Entrusted with the mission of forming a government under Wałęsa, a mission he was unable to complete. Currently a leader in the Democratic Union party.

Józef Glemp — Cardinal; Poland's primate; leader of the Catholic church in Poland.

Tadeusz Gocłowski — Bishop for Gdańsk, an influential presence in the Polish Episcopate.

Hanna Gronkiewicz-Waltz — Became head of the Polish National Bank in March 1992. A lawyer by training, specializes in financial law. Blindly devoted to Wałęsa. The leader of the tiny Victoria party, a political grouping whose sole purpose was to back Wałęsa's bid for the presidency.

Grzegorz Grzelak — Associate of Lech Wałęsa. Activist in the self-government movement. From February to November 1991 served in the president's office as secretary of state for regional self-government matters.

Andrzej Gwiazda — Founder of the Free Labor Unions. Member of the strike committee at the Gdańsk shipyard and a Solidarity leader. The main opponent and competitor to Wałęsa. Interned during martial law, he collectively spent over three years in prison. Critical of the Round Table compromise. No longer active in politics.

Aleksander Hall — Historian. Political publicist. During the 1970s the leader of the Young Poland Movement. A Solidarity and underground activist. One of the negotiators of the Round Table agreements. A minister in the government of Mazowiecki and political advisor to the prime minister. Vice-president of the Democratic Union party and leader of its right wing.

Zbigniew Janas — Communications technician. Member of the opposition and later a Solidarity member. A member of the National Commission. Cofounder of two international opposition organizations: the Polish-Czechoslovakian Solidarity and the Polish-Hungarian Solidarity. Elected representative to the Sejm. Member of the Democratic Union party.

Wojciech Jaruzelski — General and commander in chief of the Polish armed forces, now retired. The initiator and executor of a period of martial law in Poland. Author of the slogan "We shall defend Socialism as we would our own freedom." Near the end of his authoritarian rule showed political elasticity and entered into a dialogue with the opposition at the Round Table discussions. Became president of Poland as a result of the political bargain struck during the negotiations. Stepped down from office after a year and a half.

Marian Jurczyk — The leader of the Solidarność 80 trade union; ran against Wałęsa for the post of Solidarity chairman in 1981.

Jarosław Kaczyński — Twin brother of Leszek. Doctor of law. Active in the democratic opposition; Solidarity activist; a member of the Helsinki Commission and of the Citizens' Committee. One of the Round Table negotiators; senator; editor of *Tygodnik Solidarność*, taking over the post from Mazowiecki. Political advisor to Wałęsa. Chief of staff in the office of the president. Leader of the Center Alliance.

Leszek Kaczyński — Twin brother of Jarosław. Doctor of law. An activist in the independent union movement and in the democratic opposition from the early 1970s. Advisor to the strike committee at the Gdańsk shipyard. An associate of Wałęsa. Interned during martial law for his work in the underground labor unions. A negotiator at the Round Table discussions. Vice-chairman of Solidarity. Senator. Minister of security in the office of the president. Sejm deputy from the Center Alliance.

Yuri Kaszlev — Soviet ambassador to Poland who retained the post after the breakup of the Soviet Union, becoming Russia's ambassador to Poland. Initially proclaimed himself on the side of the Moscow coup leaders; later he changed his stance.

Czesław Kiszczak — General of the Polish armed forces. One of the authors of martial law. During martial law served as minister for internal security. From 1986 to 1989 a member of the Politburo attached to the Central Committee of the PZPR. One of the initiators of the Round Table negotiations, appearing on the government side. In August 1989 failed in his attempt to form a government.

Jerzu Kobylinski — Co-organizer of Wałęsa's election effort. An associate of Merkel.

Piotr Kołodziejczyk — Minister of defense in the government formed by Bielecki. A leftover from the Communist administration. Considered, with some justification, to be aligned with Wałęsa and Wachowski.

Jacek Kuroń — Educated as a historian. Author of an open letter to the Polish Communist party. Before the creation of Solidarity, spent several years in prison because of his opposition activities. The cofounder of the Workers' Defense Committee (KOR) and the Society for Educational Courses (the "Flying University"). An advisor to Solidarity. During martial law accused of an attempt to overthrow the Communist government by force. Negotiator for Solidarity at the Round Table. Minister of labor in the Mazowiecki government. Vice-chairman of the Democratic Union party. Sejm deputy.

Aleksander Kwaśniewski — Journalist, then PZPR apparachik. Government negotiator at the Round Table discussions. Leader of the Polish Social Democratic party, successor to the PZPR. Sejm deputy.

Janusz Lewandowski — Liberal minister for privatization in the government of Bielecki.

Jan Józef Lipski — an activist in the Workers' Defense Committee, a socialist, and a moral authority. Died in 1991.

Jan Lityński — part of the democratic opposition movement in the Workers' Defense Committee. An expert advisor to Solidarity. Participated in the Round Table negotiations. A member of the Democratic Union party; supporter of Mazowiecki.

Aleksander Mackiewicz — Leader of the Democratic party, which failed completely in the 1991 elections.

Henryk Majewski — Minister of internal security in the government formed by Bielecki. Holds a doctorate in engineering science. He worked at the Gdańsk Polytech in the Departments of Mechanical Engineering and Materials Testing.

Aleksander Małachowski — Writer; publicist. Sejm deputy from the leftist-oriented Solidarity Labor party. Chairman of the review committee in Solidarity.

Tadeusz Mazowiecki — Lawyer; Catholic activist. The longtime chief editor of the monthly magazine *Więź* (Link) and an elected Sejm deputy in the years of the Communist regime. An activist in the democratic opposition. Expert member of the Interenterprise Strike Committee; advisor to Lech Wałęsa and Solidarity. From 1981 the chief editor of the national weekly *Tygodnik Solidarność*. Interned during martial law. Member of the Citizens' Committee. One of the main supporters and initiators of the Round Table discussions. The first non-Communist prime minister. A candidate for the president of Poland; lost in a three-way race with Wałęsa and Tymiński. The leader of the largest party in the parliament, the Democratic Union party.

Jacek Merkel — Trained as an engineer specializing in ship construction. A member of the strike committee at the Gdańsk shipyard and of the Solidarity National Commission. Interned during martial law. Underground activist and leader of the strike in August 1988. A negotiator at the Round Table. Sejm deputy. The founder of the Solidarity Economic Foundation. Chief of the campaign staff for Wałęsa during the presidential race. A candidate for prime minister. Minister of national security in the office of the president, dismissed for unknown reasons. President of the Polish-American Solidarność-Chase Bank. Member of the Liberal Democratic Congress party.

Adam Michnik — Historian; essayist; the chief editor of *Gazeta Wyborcza*. An activist in the democratic opposition; the coorganizer of the Society for Educational Courses. Imprisoned and persecuted repeatedly by the Communists. Advisor to Solidarity. Interned during martial law and accused of an attempt to overthrow the Communist government by force. A negotiator at the Round Table. Sejm deputy.

Jerzy Milewski — Secretary of state for national security in the president's office. A former associate of Merkel. From 1981 to 1989 the chief of the Solidarity labor union foreign office in Brussels. Currently loyal to Wałęsa and Wachowski.

Leszek Miller — One of the leaders of the Polish Social Democratic party, formed from the remnants of the PZPR. Member of parliament.

Alfred Miodowicz — Longtime leader of the OPZZ. A past member of the Central Committee in the PZPR.

Zdzisław Najder — Literary historian, expert on the works of Joseph Conrad. An activist in the cause of Polish independence. Spent the time after the onset of martial law outside the country. Director of the Polish section of Radio Free Europe. Given the death sentence in absentia by the Communists for alleged cooperation with U.S. security services. Returned to Poland in 1989. Appointed by Wałęsa to steer the work of the Citizens' Committee. Advisor to Wałęsa and Prime Minister Olszewski.

Małgorzata Niezabitowska — Press spokeswoman of the Mazowiecki government. Called Wałęsa "the man who would hurry things along with an ax." Previous to this a journalist at *Tygodnik Solidarność*, where Mazowiecki had been editor before becoming prime minister.

Jan Nowak-Jeziorański — Legendary soldier of the Home Army. Performed the role of emissary for the underground Home Army command during World War II. Made five secret journeys on the Warsaw-Stockholm-London route. Remained abroad after the war acting as director of the Polish section of Radio Free Europe from 1952 to 1976. Now a resident of the United States, member of the Polish American Congress and advisor to the U.S. National Security Council.

Piotr Nowina-Konopka — Doctor of economics; Catholic activist. Associate of Lech Wałęsa during 1982–1987, later his press spokesman. Liaison between office of President Jaruzelski and Solidarity. Supported Mazowiecki's bid for the presidency. Sejm deputy and general secretary of the Democratic Union party.

Jan Olszewski — Lawyer, often acting as defense attorney in political trials, such as those of Kuroń and Michnik. An active participant in the democratic opposition. An advisor to Solidarity; author of the union's bylaws. A negotiator at the Round Table discussions. In December 1991 he was named as prime minister in a right-of-center government.

Janusz Onyszkiewicz — Deputy minister for national defense in the government of Mazowiecki. A member of the Democratic Union party. Sejm deputy. During martial law served as press spokesman for Solidarity.

Daniel Passent — Publicist and editorial writer at the weekly journal *Polityka*.

Józef Piłsudski — An activist in the cause of Polish independence; politician; marshal of Poland; a national hero. The creator of the Polish Legions, the embryonic Polish armed forces. During the World War I was interned by the Germans at Magdeburg. In November 1918 was released and returned to Poland to head the government. In 1920 the army under his command crushed the Bolshevik Red Army near Warsaw. With some initial public support, staged a coup d'état in 1926 to become the informal ruler of Poland until his death in 1935.

Krzysztof Pusz — Trained as a lawyer; an entrepreneur by avocation. Underground activist; superb organizer. From November 1987 the defacto secretary to Wałęsa, then chief of the Solidarity National Commission bureau. Under secretary of state in the office of the president.

Mieczysław Rakowski — Journalist and onetime editor in chief of the weekly *Polityka*. An activist in the Communist party. Vice–prime minister 1981–1985. The ninth, and last, Communist prime minister (1988–1989) and the final first secretary of the PZPR.

Arkadiusz Rybicki — One of the leaders of the Young Poland Movement. Interned during martial law. In the period 1983–1988 secretary to Lech Wałęsa. Under secretary of state in the office of the president and his political advisor. Coauthor of Wałęsa's book *The Struggle and the Triumph*.

Władysław Siła-Nowicki — Solidarity expert on the law; leader of the small Christian Democratic party.

Krzysztof Skubiszewski — Currently foreign minister. Survived all the previous governments—Mazowiecki's, Bielecki's, Olszewski's, and Pawlak's.

Andrzej Słowik — Solidarity activist in the city of Łódź. Vice-minister of labor in the right-oriented government of Olszewski.

Andrzej Stelmachowski — Professor of civil law; advisor to the strike committee at the Gdańsk shipyard. Advisor to Solidarity. A negotiator at the Round Table discussions. A member of the Citizens' Committee under Wałęsa. Marshal of the first postwar senate chosen by a free vote. Member of the National Defense Committee.

Stanisław Stomma —Longtime opposition member; a member of the Catholic Znak organization; a Sejm deputy while the Communists still held power. A journalist at *Tygodnik Powszechny* (Universal weekly), a Catholic publication.

Aleksander Świejkowski — Journalist working for the Polish section of Radio Free Europe.

Andrzej Szczypiorski — Writer; journalist; senator.

Jacek Taylor — Defense attorney in many political trials; a friend of Nowak-Jeziorański.

Jerzy Turowicz — Longtime chief editor of *Tygodnik Powszechny*. Dean of the opposition movement in Poland. A member of the Citizens' Committee under Wałęsa.

Stanisław Tymiński — The so-called man from nowhere. Polish emigrant who at one time resided in Peru and Canada. One of the six candidates in the presidential election of 1990. Defeated Mazowiecki and stood against Wałęsa in the resulting runoff election. Formed the populist Party X. Also known as the "Polish Ross Perot" (though probably far less clever and definitely less wealthy).

Leopold Unger — Journalist for the Belgian publication *Le Soir;* a commentator for Radio Free Europe. Emigrated from Poland in 1969.

Jerzy Urban — Journalist; editorial writer. From 1981 to 1989 the Communist government's press spokesman. Famous for saying that "the government will always manage to feed itself"; his press conferences were dubbed hate sessions by some attendees. Now the publisher and editor of a vulgar and popular publication called *Nie* (No).

Mieczysław Wachowski — Initially only Wałęsa's driver in 1980, soon became confidant and more. Imprisoned during martial law, but released after one day. Assisted the Wałęsa family until 1983 when he broke off with Wałęsa and went into the tire business. In 1989 signed on as a bosun for a round the world trip on a sailing ship. Reappeared to supplant Wałęsa's personal secretary and eventually became the cabinet chief of staff.

Jerzy Waldorff — Journalist, an activist in cultural causes.

Edward Weinert — Former commander of the Vistula units of the so-called Internal Security Corps. Regarded as an ally of Wachowski, but dismissed from his command.

Andrzej Wielowieyski — An activist in the Catholic Intelligentsia Clubs. One of the leaders of the Democratic Union party. Senator. Member of the Citizens' Committee under Wałęsa.

Piotr Wierzbicki — Conservative journalist at the *Tygodnik Solidarność*. A supporter of Wałęsa's presidency. The chief editor of *Nowy Świat* (New world), a conservative daily newspaper.

Henryk Wujec — Physicist; an activist in the democratic opposition and later in Solidarity. A member of the Solidarity National Commission. Interned and charged with an attempt to overthrow the government by force, spent many years in Communist prisons. An energetic cofounder of the Citizens' Committee and its secretary. Active in the self-government movement; member of the Democratic Union party; Sejm deputy.

Krzysztof Wyszkowski — Journalist. Active in the Gdańsk opposition movement since the mid-1970s. Met Wałęsa in the Free Labor Unions. During 1980–1981 worked with Mazowiecki on *Tygodnik Solidarność*. Went into hiding during martial law. Advisor to Wałęsa. Participated in the strikes at the Gdańsk shipyard in May and August 1988. Advisor to prime minister Olszewski.

Maciej Zalewski — Member of the Center Alliance party; associate of Jarosław Kaczynski. Sejm deputy. During the Moscow coup, chief of the National Security Bureau attached to the president's office.

Janusz Ziółkowski — Professor of sociology; minister of state, chief of staff in the president's office.

Chronology

1989

July 3 — Adam Michnik introduces the slogan "your [the Communists'] president, our [Solidarity's] prime minister."

July 19 — Wojciech Jaruzelski is chosen as president.

August 17 — A coalition of Solidarity, the ZSL, and the SD is created.

August 24 — Tadeusz Mazowiecki becomes prime minister, insisting "I am not a figurehead."

September 12 — A new cabinet is created.

September 27 — Jarosław Kaczyński becomes the new editor of *Tygodnik Solidarność*.

November 15 — Wałęsa becomes the third person in history, after Lafayette and Churchill, to give a speech before a joint session of the U.S. Congress. The ovation lasts ten minutes. Even a senator with an arm in a cast claps.

December 9–10 — A conference of the citizens' movement Etos Solidarnośći is held. Jarosław Kaczyński calls it "an attempt to create a monolithic party."

December 12 — Wałęsa appeals for the government to adopt special authority in regulating the most important areas of political and economic life in Poland; the prime minister is surprised by the proposal.

December 18 — Wałęsa attends the funeral of Andrei Sakharov.

December 20 — Wałęsa meets with Leszek Miller, the secretary of the Central Committee and Politburo member, and prepares for a talk with Mieczysław Rakowski, the first secretary of the Central Committee of the Polish Communist party.

December 30 — A private, hour-long conversation between Wałęsa and Rakowski takes place at the Sejm building. The Communists seek assurances that the Round Table agreements will hold in the future. Millions of Poles view the exchange of small talk and fish stories on television.

1990

January 8 — Workers at the Józef Piłsudski shipyard demonstrate, enraged at the meeting with Rakowski.

January 11 — In an interview with *Polityka*, Wałęsa states that "the new Communist party, the new Left, must be based on new, uncompromised people."

January 14 — In a conversation with Wałęsa, Mazowiecki mentions the proposed initiative for speeded up self-government elections.

January 16 — Wałęsa, from Gdańsk, urges speeded-up municipal elections. The prime minister accuses Wałęsa of disloyalty and theft of the idea.

January 18 — Wałęsa meets with the Soviet ambassador, Vladimir Brovikov, telling him that the USSR must remove its armed forces before the end of the year.

January 22 — Meeting with Sejm vice-marshal Tadeusz Fiszbach, Wałęsa strengthens the "left leg": He orchestrates the demolition of the PZPR.

January 25 — Wałęsa ignores Vaclav Havel's visit in Warsaw.

January 30 — Although the PZPR is dissolved, Wałęsa observes, "This is not the new Left but repainted Communists."

February 15 — The presidium of the Solidarity Executive Committee, together with Lech Wałęsa, meets with members of the government and Mazowiecki.

February 22 — Zdzisław Najder is named the leader of the Citizens' Committee under the head of the Solidarity labor union.

February 27 — Adam Michnik comes to Gdańsk.

March 12 — Wałęsa sends a congratulatory letter to Vyautas Landsbergis on the date Lithuania regains its independence. "I trust that the Lithuanian nation, which for years maintained its separateness, will show understanding to similar desires among the Poles living in Lithuania."

March 17 — Havel and Wałęsa meet at a chalet in the Karkonosze Mountains.

March 28 — In an interview with *Elsevier*, Wałęsa says Germany "will be blown off the map" if it tries to destabilize Europe.

March 31 — The Citizens' Committee in Warsaw is enlarged by twenty-two new members. Wałęsa aims a strong statement at Mazowiecki and the government criticizing the sluggish pace of reforms: "We are sentimentalists. We do not issue decrees!"

April 2 — "If I had to choose again, I would again choose Mazowiecki," Wałęsa tells workers at a meeting in Pruszcz Gdański.

April 10 — Wałęsa confirms that he will seek the office of the president.

April 19–24 — The Second National Solidarity Congress is held.

April 21 — Wałęsa is elected union leader with 362 votes (77.5 percent).

April 26 — At a press conference Wałęsa apologizes to Jaruzelski "for the style of discussion on the subject of the presidency."

May 4 — Richard von Weizsäcker, president of the Federal Republic of Germany visits Gdańsk. He shows no interest in Wałęsa's monologue.

May 9 — Cyrus Vance, former U.S. secretary of state, talks with Wałęsa on the subject of "war of everyone against everyone else." Vance is not able even to feign a smile.

May 12 — The Center Alliance is created.

May 13 — At a meeting of the Citizens' Committee, Wałęsa declares, "We need a war on the top so that we can have peace at the lower levels. Today my vacation is over."

May 28 — Wałęsa negotiates an end to the Słupsk rail strike, which started on May 10.

June 1 — Wałęsa writes to Citizens' Committee secretary Henryk Wujec: "Consider yourself dismissed."

June 4 — Wałęsa tries to oust Michnik from his post as editor in chief of the *Gazeta Wyborcza*.

June 5 — At a meeting with cardinal Agostino Casaroli at the nuncio's residence in Warsaw, Wałęsa receives a cool embrace from the prime minister.

June 8 — "I don't want to be president; I will have to be president," Wałęsa tells an interviewer from the *Gazeta Wyborcza*.

June 11 — Wałęsa accepts the Center Alliance, giving it his full support.

June 12 — Congressman Dan Rostenkowski visits Gdańsk, the trip a reaction to Wałęsa's conversation with Vance a month before. He wants a private conference; Wałęsa insists that he has no secrets before the press. Rostenkowski's message: business needs political stability.

June 13 — Again in Słupsk, Wałęsa discusses the results of the government negotiations with the rail workers. Emotions are at a zenith.

June 14–16 — At a session of the International Labour Organisation in Geneva, Wałęsa claims someone is trying to involve him in a conflict with the prime minister.

June 16 — Wałęsa meets with protesting farmers from the Mława milk cooperative who have been blocking the road between Warsaw and Gdańsk for several days. After a sharp three-hour discussion, the tractors pull off the road.

June 19 — Wałęsa meets with Polish Peasant party leader Roman Bartoszcze and Aleksander Mackiewicz in Gdańsk. The nearly forgotten Solidarity-PSL-SD coalition is mentioned. Wałęsa is in control.

June 21 — Henry Kissinger, former U.S. secretary of state, arrives in Gdańsk and appeals for unity between the Warsaw and Gdańsk factions.

June 22 — Małgorzata Niezabitowska, the government press spokeswoman, makes a mocking remark about Wałęsa's "hurrying things up with an ax."

June 24 — At a drama-filled meeting of the Citizens' Committee, a letter signed by sixty-three members is presented. It calls for the dissolution of the committee. Wałęsa calls this a betrayal.

June 30 — Mazowiecki has his first defeat—victory for Wałęsa. The great majority of representatives from local citizens' committees support Wałęsa's concept of flexibility in the structure of the committees.

July 2 — Wałęsa invites Mazowiecki to a meeting at the Gdańsk shipyard on July 8 to patch up their differences.

July 4 — The prime minister refuses to go to Gdańsk, suggesting that Wałęsa and he take advantage of Archbishop Dąbrowski's offer to use a cloister near Warsaw instead.

July 7 — During their discussion, neither Wałęsa nor Mazowiecki backs down: Mazowiecki does not want Wałęsa to run for president; Wałęsa insists that he will.

July 8 — A meeting of the OKP parliamentarians and representatives of the Solidarity committees from enterprises in the Tri-City area. Many accusations are hurled at the government. During the intermission Wałęsa meets with the members of the delegation from the Liberal Democratic Congress who tell him: "Within two weeks you can be the man inside Belweder Palace."

August 31 — The tenth anniversary of Solidarity. At the bishop's residence in Gdańsk, another meeting takes place between Wałęsa and Mazowiecki. "Let us be opponents, not enemies," says the prime minister.

September 10 — Schewach Weiss, vice-marshal of the Knesset, visits Gdańsk. "I proved that I was not an anti-Semite," says Wałęsa; "I believe him," answers Weiss.

September 17 — Wałęsa announces his candidacy for the presidency.

September 18 — At the cardinal's residence a meeting takes place for representatives of all the major political groups. Wałęsa and Mazowiecki have a final conversation. All self-deception ends; there is no common toast.

October 5 — Mazowiecki decides to seek the presidency.

November 25 — Mazowiecki is eliminated in the first round of elections. Wałęsa's opponent in the second round is the "man from nowhere," Stanisław Tymiński.

December 9 — Wałęsa is elected president.

December 12 — The president-elect occupies temporary headquarters in Sopot after resigning from his position as head of the Solidarity labor union.

December 22 — The swearing-in ceremony takes place before the parliament. Wałęsa becomes commander in chief of the armed forces, receives the insignia of his office, and is installed at the Belweder Palace.

1991

January 9 — Wałęsa appoints Franciszek Cybula, his personal confessor, as presidential chaplain.

February 5 — Wałęsa visits Italy and the Vatican, meeting with the president of the Italian republic and the pope.

February 14 — The president supports the nomination of post-Communist Sejm deputy Wiesława Ziółkowska as head of the inspector general's office. The Sejm, however, rejects her with an overwhelming majority of votes.

February 15 — Wałęsa signs the so-called Triangular Agreement, a treaty of cooperation between Poland, Hungary, and Czechoslovakia.

February 16 — Cardinal Glemp, the Polish primate, consecrates a chapel at the Belweder Palace.

March 12 — Jacek Merkel is suddenly and mysteriously relieved of his post as minister for state security.

March 19–28 — Wałęsa visits the United States, meeting with President Bush and former president Ronald Reagan.

April 3–4 — Wałęsa makes a state visit to Belgium.

April 9 — Wałęsa meets with François Mitterrand, president of France.

April 23–26 — Wałęsa makes a state visit to Great Britain.

May 3 — The president participates in celebrating the bicentennial of the Polish Third of May Constitution.

May 20 — Wałęsa meets with Israeli president Chaim Herzog and delivers a speech of reconciliation before the Knesset in which he apologizes for Polish anti-Semitism.

June 8 — Pope John Paul II is a guest at Belweder Palace.

June 26 — The president refuses to sign legislation that would regulate the election process for candidates to the Polish Sejm. This is the beginning of the dispute between the president and parliament over rules governing future elections.

July 2–3 — Wałęsa visits NATO headquarters. Minister Mieczysław Wachowski edits the parts of Wałęsa's speech that could be interpreted as anti-Russian.

August 19 — An attempted coup in Moscow leads to indecision and inaction in the Belweder.

August 21 — Wałęsa conducts phone conversations with Boris Yeltsin and Havel.

August 28 — Wałęsa telephones Mikhail Gorbachev.

September 6 — The heads of the three Triangular Agreement countries meet.

October 27 — Parliamentary elections are held.

October 30–31 — Key members of the president's staff are dismissed. Among them are Arkadiusz Rybicki, Krzysztof Pusz, Jarosław Kaczyński, Leszek Kaczyński, Grzegorz Grzelak, and Maciej Zalewski.

December 5 — Wałęsa speaks before the newly elected Sejm. He nominates Jan Olszewski for the post of prime minister.

1992

March 5 — After several attempts, Lech Wałęsa manages to force through the appointment of Hanna Gronkiewicz-Waltz as president of the Polish National Bank.

March 29 — President Lech Wałęsa makes a state visit to Germany.

May 6 — Presidents Lech Wałęsa, Vaclav Havel, and Prime Minister Jozsef Antall meet in Kraków. A free trade zone is announced for the Triangular Agreement countries.

May 22 — Lech Wałęsa and Russian President Boris Yeltsin sign a treaty of friendship and cooperation in Moscow. The signing is preceded by an announcement condemning Stalin's crimes and totalitarianism. Prime Minister Olszewski sends a secret dispatch to Wałęsa in Moscow, protesting the wording of the Polish-Russian treaty. A major political dispute begins between the government and the president.

June 4 — The Sejm, on the president's request, dismisses Prime Minister Olszewski. The new prime minister is Waldemar Pawlak, leader of the Polish Peasant party.

During the stormy Sejm session the president is handed a list, created by the Ministry of Internal Affairs, containing the names of high government officials accused of collaboration with the security services of the former Communist government.

July 10 — Prime Minister Pawlak fails to form a government. He is replaced by Hanna Suchocka, a member of the Democratic Union party.

October 4 — Lech Wałęsa travels to Nowy Sącz, a city in the south of Poland, to take part in a celebration commemorating its 700 year anniversary. (It was in Nowy Sącz that Wałęsa received the most votes during the presidential election).

October 17 — The Sejm approves the so-called "little constitution," which affirms its control over the armed forces, but takes away the right to dissolve government.

November 12 — The president submits a legislative project to the Sejm, a bill of rights and freedoms, as a supplement to the "little constitution."

December 7 — Lech Wałęsa officially expresses his concern over the situation in Śląsk Opolski, where activities among the German minority have taken on some controversial forms (Nazi symbols and traditions).

December 12 — Photographs of Sejm deputies in the act of voting "with two hands" (for their absent colleagues) appear in the media. Wałęsa calls it a political scandal.

December 15 — Polish television again airs the Wałęsa-Miodowicz debate of 1988. Commentators respond with criticism.

About the Book

Drawing on his unique insider's perspective as press spokesman for Lech Wałęsa from October 1989 to July 1990, Jarosław Kurski has written the first critical, clear-eyed account of the Polish leader's personal and political style. During his time in Wałęsa's office, Kurski became acquainted with the many forces and ambitions—which were unknown to the general public—that drove the Solidarity hero as Poland shed its Communist rulers. Challenging conventional hagiography, Kurski criticizes Wałęsa's political modus operandi, arguing that the leader manipulated or alienated many of his old supporters—including Tadeusz Mazowiecki, the man Wałęsa had championed as the first postwar non-Communist prime minister of Poland. While crediting Wałęsa's many accomplishments, the author paints a damning portrait of a man losing touch with both the political situation and the working people who brought him to power.

Through extensive interviews with many of Wałęsa's current and past associates, Kurski bolsters his own conclusions while providing a multifaceted picture of Walesa and of the events that propelled him to the presidency of Poland.

Jarosław Kurski is a journalist living in Poland. **Peter Obst** is a freelance translator and journalist whose articles have appeared in the *Wall Street Journal Europe* and the *Polish American Journal.*

Index